DOROTHY THOMPSON was born in 1923 and grew up in London and France. She graduated in history from Girton College, Cambridge in 1945, having interrupted her studies with war service as an engineering draughtswoman. In 1948 she married and while her three children were young, worked part-time in adult education and on various sociological surveys. Since 1968 she has worked in the History Department at Birmingham University, apart from spells as a visiting professor at Rutgers, Pittsburgh and Brown Universities in the USA. She has worked mainly on popular politics and the social history of nineteenth-century Britain and Ireland. The author of several books and articles, her most recent work is the highly acclaimed *The Chartists* (1984). She has been active in the peace movement for many years, and edited the collection *Over Our Dead Bodies: Women Against the Bomb* (Virago, 1983). She now lives in Worcester with her husband, the historian E. P. Thompson.

PLEASE RETURN TO:

Bandung Limited
Block H
Carker's Lane
53-79 Highgate Road
London
NW5 1TL

Telephone
071*482 5045

Facsimile
071*284 0930

D0319109

Dorothy Thompson

QUEEN
VICTORIA

GENDER AND POWER

Published by VIRAGO PRESS Limited 1990
20–23 Mandela Street, Camden Town, London NW1 0HQ

Copyright © 1990 Dorothy Thompson

*A CIP Catalogue record for this book
is available from the British Library*

Typeset by Goodfellow & Egan, Cambridge

Printed in Great Britain by
Billing & Sons Limited, Worcester.

DEDICATION

IT is not usual to dedicate a biography to anyone other than its subject. Since this is not strictly speaking a biography, but is partly a study of parallel lives, I should like to associate in its dedication my great-grandmother, Anne Coleman, whom I remember well. She was born in 1837, the year in which Victoria came to the throne, into a family of East London silk-weavers. She too was widowed in her early forties, but brought up and educated her five children by her own and her children's earnings.

CONTENTS

LIST OF ILLUSTRATIONS

ACKNOWLEDGEMENTS

THIS book was originally designed as one of the Virago *Pioneers*, a series intended to spotlight outstanding nineteenth-century women in a popular and accessible way. It has slipped out of the series, but retains the format, being an attempt at reinterpretation rather than fresh scholarship.

As will be clear to readers, my greatest debt is to the many scholars who have already worked in this field. I have tried to acknowledge all those from whom I actually took material, but there were dozens more books and articles which helped me to get what insight I have managed to gain into the extraordinary world of Britain's longest-reigning monarch. There is no space to list them all, but if any authors feel I have lifted material without acknowledgement, please forgive me.

The interpretation and the howlers are my own, but a number of people have helped with discussions and with references and ideas. Again I can list only a few. My husband, Edward, who has also long been fascinated by the Empress Brown, has helped in innumerable ways, and our daughter Kate patiently read the script and made many useful comments. Robin Blackburn, Alf Jenkins, Angela Lambert and Ben Pimlott have all given valuable suggestions. Sections of the book have been tried out as papers at Queen's University, Kingston, Ontario and at the University of Toronto, in both cases producing valuable comments and discussion. A paper given to graduate students at a seminar organized by Nev Kirk of Manchester Polytechnic elicited, as well as helpful comments, the only example I have so far discovered of a 'John Brown' street song, unfortunately unprintable, but illustrating the persistence of an oral tradition.

I am grateful to the Oxford University Press for permission to reproduce the extracts from the letters of Lord Macaulay from their 1961 edition of Macaulay's *Life and Letters*, edited by Sir George Otto Trevelyan; to Evans Brothers for permission to quote from the volumes of correspondence between Queen Victoria and her daughter, edited by Sir Roger Fulford; to Her Majesty The Queen for her gracious permission for the republication of material from the Royal Archives which is subject to copyright; and to the authors and publishers of two important modern works: Angela Lambert's *Unquiet Souls* (London, Macmillan, 1984) for permission to reproduce some of the Scawen Blunt diary, and Michaela Reid's *Ask Sir James* (London, Hodder and Stoughton, 1987), from which I have taken some extracts from the diary of Sir James Reid. Both these books contain a great many insights into the whole period. The cartoons on pp. 88, 102, 111, 129, are reproduced by courtesy of *Punch*.

THE ROYAL FAMILY

A select list of members who are mentioned in this book

George III (1738–1820), ruled 1760–1820, had nine sons and six daughters, including (in order of age)

1. George, Prince of Wales (1762–1830). Regent 1812–1820, King George IV 1820–1830. Married (1795) Caroline of Brunswick. They had one daughter, Charlotte (1796–1817), who married (1816) Leopold of Saxe-Coburg, and died in childbirth.

2. Frederick, Duke of York (1763–1827). No children.

3. William Henry, Duke of Clarence (1765–1837). William IV 1830–1837. No legitimate children (10 others).

5. Edward Augustus, Duke of Kent (1767–1820). Married (1818) Victoria, widowed sister of Leopold of Saxe-Coburg, who already had two children by her first marriage to the Prince of Leinigen. These two, Charles and Feodora, were half-siblings of her daughter by the Duke of Kent, Victoria (1819–1901), who ruled 1837–1901. The Duchess of Kent's other brother, Ernest of Saxe-Coburg-Gotha, was the father of Albert, Prince Consort to Queen Victoria (1819–1861).

8. Ernest Augustus (1771–1851). King of Hanover 1837–1851. His son George V of Hanover (1819–1878) ruled until deposed in 1866.

9. Augustus Frederick, Duke of Sussex (1773–1843). No children.

10. Adolphus Frederick, Duke of Cambridge (1774–1850). Three children, including George (1819–1904), who was Chief of Staff for most of Victoria's reign, and Mary Adelaide, whose daughter, Mary, married King George V, Victoria's grandson.

George III's older sister, Augusta (1737–1813) married Charles, Prince of Brunswick. Caroline of Brunswick, their daughter, married George IV (see above), who was her first cousin.

Queen Victoria's children

1 Victoria Adelaide Mary Louise (1840–1901), Princess Royal (Vicky). Married (1858) Prince Frederick William of Prussia. Three sons and four daughters. Her eldest son became Kaiser Wilhelm II.

2 Albert Edward (1841–1910), Prince of Wales (Bertie). Married (1863) Alexandra, daughter of King Christian of Denmark. Reigned as Edward VII, 1901–1910. Three sons, three daughters.

3 Alice Mary Maud (1843–1878). Married Prince Frederick William Louis of Hesse Darmstadt. Two sons, five daughters.

4 Alfred Ernest Albert (1844–1900), Duke of Edinburgh and Duke of Coburg (Affie). Married (1874) Grand Duchess Maria Alexandrovna of Russia. One son, four daughters.

5 Helena Augusta Victoria (1846–1923), (Lenchen). Married (1866) Prince Christian of Schleswig-Holstein. Three sons, two daughters.

6 Louise Caroline Alberta (1848–1939). Married (1871) John Campbell, Marquess of Lorne, later ninth Duke of Argyll. No children.

7 Arthur William Patrick Albert (1850–1942), Duke of Connaught, Governor-General of Canada 1911–1916. Married (1879) Princess Louisa Margaret, daughter of Prince Frederick Karl of Prussia. One son, two daughters.

8 Leopold George Duncan Albert (1853–1884), Duke of Albany. A semi-invalid, born with haemophilia. Married (1881) Helen Frederika Augusta of Waldeck-Pyrmont. One son, one daughter.

9 Beatrice Mary Victoria Feodora (1857–1944), (Baby). Married (1885) Henry Prince of Battenberg. Two sons, one daughter.

VICTORIA'S PRIME MINISTERS

1837–1841	William Lamb, Lord Melbourne	*Whig*
1841–1846	Sir Robert Peel	*Tory*
1846–1852	Lord John Russell	*Whig*
1852–	Lord Derby	*Tory*
1852–1855	Lord Aberdeen	*coalition Whig/Peelite*
1855–1858	William Temple, Lord Pamerston	*Whig*
1858–1859	Lord Derby	*Tory*
1859–1865	Lord Palmerston	*Whig*
1865–1866	Lord John Russell	*Liberal*
1866–1868	Lord Derby/Benjamin Disraeli	*Conservative*
1868–1874	William Ewart Gladstone	*Liberal*
1874–1880	Benjamin Disraeli	*Conservative*
1880–1885	Gladstone	*Liberal*
1885–1886	Lord Salisbury	*Conservative*
1886–	Gladstone	
1886–1892	Lord Salisbury	
1892–1894	Gladstone	
1894–1895	Lord Rosebery	*Liberal*
1895–1901	Lord Salisbury	

INTRODUCTION:
ENGLAND IN 1837

VICTORIA'S was the longest reign of any British monarch. She came to the throne when the British royal house was running out of legitimate candidates for its occupation. By the time of her death her nine children, thirty-six grandchildren and thirty-seven great-grandchildren, with their spouses, constituted a flock of Battenbergs, Bernadottes, Bourbons, Bourbon-Parmas, Braganças, Coburgs, Glucksburgs, Hapsburgs, Hesses, Hohenzollerns, Mecklenburg-Strelitzes, Romanovs, Savoys and Wittenbachs, enough to occupy most of the remaining thrones of Europe for the foreseeable future. She came to the throne almost without resources, still burdened indeed by her father's debts. She died one of the richest women in Europe and head of one of the world's richest families. She acceded to a throne under threat from popular republicanism and ultra-right absolutism and left it secure enough to survive a half-century of war, depression and scandal until the advent of another female sovereign continued and reinforced the trends her reign had set in motion.

Victoria occupied the throne from 1837 to 1901, reigning for nearly two-thirds of the nineteenth century. Thousands of volumes have been written about the events of those years, and there will doubtless be many more. This short study cannot attempt to cover even the main events of the queen's life, let alone the lives of her subjects. Instead, it will explore some of the moments when the fact that a woman was on the throne seems to be of particular significance during a century in which women were increasingly discouraged from taking part in the public life of the country. It is an odd contradiction that in the period in which the doctrine of separate spheres of activity for men and women was most actively developed and propounded, the highest public office in the land was held by a woman.

There are many controversies about the social and political history of nineteenth-century Britain, but there is little dispute about the magnitude of the changes which the century witnessed. The fashion lately is to emphasize continuities rather than to make claims for revolutionary change; there are historians who question the once accepted view that the reign of Victoria marked a sharp break with the style and traditions of the early Hanoverians. Her reign began at the height of what was once seen as the first industrial revolution, and here again there are historians who stress continuities in Britain's industrial development rather than seeing the first four decades of the century as being disrupted by conflicts between tradition and innovation in industry, between workers defending their customary status and a new breed of employer anxious to rush through technological change. Whether the changes taking place in Britain were revolutionary and disruptive, or were simply the continuation of longer-term movements, however, it must be recognized that Victoria came to the throne in a period of social, political and economic turbulence.

The 1830s and 1840s in Britain were political decades. George Eliot, looking back from the 1860s, described the age as one 'when faith in the efficacy of political change was at fever-heat in ardent reformers' and went on to say that 'such a time is a time of hope'. It was the atmosphere of hope and the faith in peaceful political change which led liberal and radical politicians, even those who inclined towards republican views, to welcome the advent of a new, young monarch who contrasted in every way – age, gender and political loyalty – with her unpopular predecessors.

The overall optimism which informed radical politics, in spite of many areas of bitterness and revolt, rested on two major pieces of legislation which had apparently been achieved by peaceful mass popular action, the Catholic Emancipation Act of 1829 and the Reform Bill of 1832. A campaign among Irish electors and non-electors had sent a Catholic candidate, Daniel O'Connell, back repeatedly to the House of Commons, where he was debarred from sitting by his refusal to take an oath abjuring the main articles of his religion; his persistent return had forced an entirely Protestant House of Commons to abolish the oath and to admit Catholics to almost every public office, the exceptions being those of the monarch or regent, Lord Chancellor and Lord Lieutenant of Ireland. Three years later, a House of Commons composed entirely of members elected on a franchise based on landed property, and a House of Lords made up of the great landowners of Britain, responded to public pressure and extended the franchise to admit men whose property was in trade or business concerns, including some indeed who owned no property but whose income enabled them to occupy a house worth £10 a year in rent. The Duke of Wellington described the Reform Bill as 'the revolution', and it did indeed seem to many that Britain, alone among the great powers of Europe, had seen the downfall of the *ancien régime* without significant violence. To those for whom the reforms did not go far enough – the Irish who wanted a complete repeal of the union with England, and the radicals who wanted the suffrage extended to all male citizens – the achievements of these two 'instalments' of reform inspired hopes of greater achievements by the same methods.

The first ten years of Victoria's reign saw the acting out of these campaigns – especially, on the British mainland, by the Chartist movement for universal adult male suffrage, whose petitions and demonstrations involved more people during the decade than any other popular movement in the whole of the century. In spite of the scale of these demonstrations, however, Britain alone among the great powers of Europe did not experience a revolutionary uprising in 1848 of a sufficient scale to topple, or even to threaten, the existing government. Here again the special conditions which told against revolutionary action in Britain included the gender of the monarch. As George Eliot put it, 'Our little humbug of a queen is more endurable than the rest of her race because she calls forth a chivalrous feeling', but she mentioned the additional factor that 'there is nothing in our constitution to obstruct the slow progress of *political* reform.'

In the course of this book I shall look for the reasons for the stability of the British power structure, in particular the throne, during this period of turbulence. By the mid-century faith in political action had declined dramatically. Theories came into favour which stressed the primacy of economic causes for social ills, particularly the doctrines of Free Trade and *laisser-faire*. In 1846 the Corn Laws, which protected home-grown grains from competition with cheaper imported ones, were repealed in what was apparently a victory for commercial over landed interests. The prosperity which followed – in fact unconnected with the repeal – lent strength to arguments against political intervention in areas of trade and employment, and led to the development of institutions, from trade unions to building societies, which enabled people to protect their own interests in narrower and more localized ways. The experience of France disillusioned many political radicals, who saw a political revolution that had failed to solve the social problems and attempts at political and social emancipation that had been defeated partly by force but partly by the very panacea of manhood suffrage itself, which had resulted in the election of a reactionary head of state. French example also strengthened popular monarchism, for the constitutionally controlled figure of the young queen and her family offered a reassuring contrast to the ambitious imperialism of the head of the French state.

In 1837, Victoria ruled over a nation which was divided by questions of religion, nationality and property. Several millions of her subjects within the British Isles, in Wales, Scotland and Ireland, did not speak English and were therefore outside the main stream of politics for most purposes. None of her female subjects and only a very small number of her male ones had any direct voice in the politics of the country, whose local and national governmental institutions were controlled by a comparatively small number of very wealthy families, and in the localities by the lesser landed gentry and a narrowly-based group of urban property-owners. The Reform Bill had opened up the possibility of the correction of some of these injustices and inequalities, and indeed in the years between it and her accession a number of sweeping administrative reforms had been passed, including the rationalization of urban local government and the total reorganization of the patchy and in many cases corrupt system of poor relief.

Unfortunately for the poorer members of society, most of the reforms of the 1830s resulted only in the admission to areas of power of some of the new voters, who were in many cases the industrialists, merchants and employers. The conflicts within the nation switched from being between the 'excluded' and the monopolizing 'landed interest' of the pre-reform period to being between the 'excluded' – now only the propertyless – and the empowered groups which represented all kinds of property. Less than a decade into Victoria's reign, Disraeli, then a young novelist just embarking on a political career, put into the mouth of a Chartist character in one of his books the famous contention that the queen reigned over two nations,

> between whom there is no intercourse and no sympathy; who are as ignorant of each other's habits, thoughts and feelings as if they were dwellers in different zones, or inhabitants of different planets: who are formed by a different breeding, are fed by a different food, are ordered by different manners, and are not governed by the same laws . . . The rich and the poor.

In 1837 both nations to some extent claimed the queen on their side.

The politics in which the British engaged in 1837 should not be confused with modern party politics. The reins of government and access to any part of the political system were controlled by a small, rich and closely connected group of families who acted as power brokers in matters of national policy and in the important area of patronage and influence. It was a historical accident, and an odd one, that a character as basically conservative and anti-democratic as Lord Melbourne, the Prime Minister at the time of Victoria's accession, should have been the leader of the reforming party. But once the Reform Bill had been passed his party, the Whigs, were as adamantly opposed to further reform as their opponents, the Tories. To the non-electors the difference between the parties was often difficult to distinguish.

The throne was seen traditionally as mediating between the different interests in the country, and the fact that Victoria, unlike her Hanoverian uncles, was associated with the Whigs and reform rather than with the Tories and absolute reaction, gave some encouragement to the excluded classes. But her youth and gender were probably more important symbols of hope for her subjects, and helped to reconcile many to traditional monarchical loyalties which, it should be remembered, included a strong folk memory – perhaps more a mythology – of good times for England under previous women rulers, from Boadicea through Good Queen Bess to Queen Anne.

1

THREE PRINCESSES

PRINCESS ALEXANDRINA VICTORIA was born on 24 May 1819, in England, her birth being witnessed and attested according to traditional royal custom. Her father, the Duke of Kent, was present throughout the birth, which was supervised by a qualified woman *accoucheuse*, Madame Siebold. The Archbishop of Canterbury, the Duke of Wellington, the Bishop of London and other notables attended in an adjoining room. At the time of her birth she was third in line of succession to the throne, her uncles the Prince Regent (soon to be George IV) and the Duke of Clarence (later William IV) coming before her. William, with a new young wife, was confidently expected to produce legitimate children to succeed him.

The circumstances of Victoria's birth were important for her later development. She was close enough to the succession to be an object of concern to the government and the royal family, which meant that she was brought up in England. Had there been more young royals in the picture her mother, who was a German princess with two children by her first (German) husband might have taken her back to Germany to be educated. As it was her governess was German and the young princess did not begin to speak English until she was three. Her mother never spoke the language with fluency, and the royal household remained bilingual. In 1839 Victoria sympathized with Lord Melbourne, the Prime Minister, for having to put up with royal conversations around him in a language which he did not understand, while in the 1860s the Scotsman John Brown taught himself German so that he could understand what the members of the royal family were talking about. Edward VII was said to have spoken English with a German accent throughout his life. Among Victoria's many gifts, however, was an excellent ear, and she seems always to have managed her two languages without difficulty. Her early education was left, for good or ill, largely in the hands of her mother for the first decade of her life.

William IV's daughters died in infancy, and on his death in 1837 Victoria succeeded him on the throne of Great Britain and Ireland. At eighteen she had just attained her majority as a ruler, although she was still legally a minor in other respects. Two of her younger uncles had produced sons in the same year as she herself had been born, and three of her father's younger brothers were still alive.

Thus, by a series of historical accidents, Victoria attained the throne as an adult, not requiring a regent; yet she was still unmarried, and so not connected in the public mind with any other royal family. Her upbringing had been comparatively secluded and for the most part free of the family feuds and intrigues in which her predecessors had been involved. Her close confidantes and advisers included her mother – a woman of many unlovable characteristics no doubt and not totally immune from scandal, but one nevertheless whose moral and familial attitudes erred on the side of strictness rather than laxity – and her uncle Leopold, her mother's brother.

The Duchess of Kent, her mother, was never popular with the British people, and was often at odds with her royal relatives. She was considered to be too much under the influence of the Comptroller of her household, a rather sinister Irishman called Sir John Conroy, who was alleged – on apparently rather slender evidence – to be her lover. Because of the mutual suspicion between her mother and her uncles, Victoria was not as close to the other members of the royal family as might have been expected, especially after it became clear that she was likely to inherit the throne.

The place of her father, who died when she was an infant, was to some extent taken by her mother's brother, Prince Leopold. He had lived mainly in England since the death of his wife Princess Charlotte, and his house was always remembered with affection by Victoria. He was liberal in outlook, serious, and very fond of his niece. Their letters on political matters show how much she looked to him for advice, and he was prepared to offer it. In 1830, after the

Belgians broke with Holland and set up their own government, Leopold accepted the invitation to become their king, and occupied the throne until his death in 1866. His liberal attitudes and the fact that he took the throne of a state which had been created as part of the liberal nationalist movement that was stirring throughout Europe made observers in Britain see his influence on the queen as being more enlightened than any she might have been subject to from her father's family. Leopold's influence and her own political inclinations at this time, as far as they were known, must have made Victoria more acceptable to a broader section of public opinion than the immediate alternatives among her uncles and cousins. Coming after 'an imbecile, a profligate and a buffoon', as the three kings who preceded her have been described, she had much in her favour.

Victoria added to the advantages of her background considerable qualities of her own. It is impossible to read her letters and journals and the accounts of contemporaries without recognizing the unusual gifts which she possessed. Her early training had taught her to harness her considerable energy and intelligence and to develop a degree of discipline and application which might well not have emerged had her future role been evident from her earliest years. A more indulgent upbringing might have had the effect of encouraging her wilfulness and obstinacy, characteristics which were evident in any case throughout her life, but which remained below the pathological level for most of the time. She had qualities of imagination and humour and, in her early years at least, qualities of sympathy and perception which have not always emerged in the conventional picture. Inevitably in her sixty years on the throne she was to become something of a monster; nevertheless, the detailed record which even the weeded versions of her journals and letters presents shows a character whom it is impossible at times not to view with sympathy and admiration.

The circumstances of her accession were therefore in many ways favourable to the young queen. Some, however, of the particular considerations which determined the character of Victoria's reign dated from well before her birth. In particular, the hopes and expectations of her subjects when she came to the throne were influenced by the lives of two earlier princesses, with neither of whom was she ever in contact.

Her first cousin Princess Charlotte, only 'legitimate' child of George IV, died before Victoria was born. Indeed, had she not died it is extremely unlikely that Victoria herself would ever have been born, since it was the death of the heir to the throne that sent the king's middle-aged brothers scuttling around to be first to provide an alternative. Charlotte's mother, Princess Caroline, survived her daughter by a few years, dying when Victoria was two years old. The lives of these two royal women were of the greatest importance to Victoria.

George, as Prince of Wales, acted as regent for his father during the last years of George III's reign, when the old king was incapacitated by madness. Popular attitudes to the monarchy fluctuated wildly during the regency and George's accession as George IV in 1820 was accompanied by scandal and tragedy. The manners and behaviour of the last two male Hanoverian monarchs undoubtedly helped to predispose sections of the British population towards a new monarch who was young and female.

British hostility to particular monarchs has tended to take the form not of outright republicanism but of support for alternative candidates for the throne. In the eighteenth century there had undoubtedly been some popular support for Jacobitism – loyalty to the legitimate Stuart line against their Hanoverian replacements. The Stuarts, however, were not very satisfactory candidates for popular support. Support for a Catholic monarchy was problematic at best in a century when Catholic massacres of Protestants – such as the massacre of St Bartholomew of 1572, which had begun the flow of French Huguenot refugees to Britain, and many subsequent episodes of such slaughter – held something of the place in English popular imagination that is today held by the Nazi Holocaust. The Stuarts were a poor lot in personal terms as well, so that although the Highlanders in Scotland and some Irish Catholics retained a somewhat mystical attachment to the line, anti-Hanoverian feeling in the rest of Britain tended to take the form of apathy, boredom and cynicism rather than support for any visible alternative. It has been suggested that in his old age George III became enormously popular, and it seems to have been the case that sheer longevity and the super-patriotism aroused during the wars against France allowed the

old king to be seen as a father-figure and an inspiration for patriotic
loyalty.

George's sons, however, soon dissipated any good will which their
father had managed to attract. The contempt with which George IV
was treated by contemporary cartoonists and pamphleteers would
amaze even the readers of today's tabloid press, whilst William IV,
though faring slightly better than his brother, was lampooned in
press and print and hooted by the crowd when he drove through
London. Had a third brother succeeded William, it is by no means
impossible to imagine that even the British people, addicted though
they have always been to the idea of kingship and the royal image,
might have preferred, in the age of reform and revolution in Europe,
to opt for some form of republican government – especially since the
next in line was the most unpopular of all George III's sons, Ernest
Augustus, Duke of Cumberland.

George, Prince of Wales and heir apparent, had produced no
legitimate offspring, but his father's failing health and the need to
rally the populace in support of expensive and painful foreign
policies emphasized the need for a clear royal line to whom allegiance
could be rallied. In return for the cancellation of his enormous debts
he agreed to take a suitable bride and produce an heir. Like most of
his brothers, he had already taken a wife. He had been married since
1785 to Mrs Fitzherbert, by whom he had several children. But this
marriage was secret and, in the light of the Royal Marriage Act of
1772, illegal. A further complication lay in the fact that Mrs
Fitzherbert was a Catholic as well as a commoner, and marriage to a
Catholic would have prevented George from succeeding to the throne
under the Act of Settlement of 1700. George was well known to be
extravagant and self-indulgent to an inordinate degree, but his
acceptance of a royal bride – his cousin, Caroline of Brunswick – and
perhaps even more the birth in 1796 of a daughter Charlotte, who
was directly in line to the throne, made her father more acceptable to
the population.

Certainly the young princess seems to have been extremely
popular – even radicals and republicans reserved their attacks for her
parents. Both parents presented splendid targets. They separated
after Charlotte's birth and soon provided food for gossip, squibs and

satires. The young princess was used by both parents as a pawn, from the earliest days of their separation. In 1806 and 1813 the Prince Regent set up 'delicate investigations' into his wife's conduct, with the view of obtaining a divorce. Neither attempt succeeded, but the bitterness between the couple was intensified by his behaviour. Princess Caroline was certainly not a model of refinement or modesty, but most people probably agreed with Princess Charlotte, who wrote to Baron Stockmar, 'My mother was bad, but she would not have become as bad as she was if my father had not been infinitely worse.'

As the years went by, the household of Princess Caroline became something of a centre for radical politicians, happy to take her side against her increasingly unpopular husband. How far Princess Charlotte seriously embraced the radical politics of her mother's circle is far from clear, although her husband, Prince Leopold of Saxe-Coburg, to whom she was married in 1816, was certainly attached to the Liberal end of the spectrum of high politics. But well before her marriage Maria Edgeworth reported an incident in which the young princess seriously annoyed her grandmother, the old Queen Charlotte.

> To provoke the Queen the Princess hung up in her apartment at Windsor a cameo of Brougham and another of Sir S. Romilly on each side of a bust of Fox. The Queen, the moment she saw them broke the cameos to pieces. Silly! silly! Was it not?

Brougham and Romilly were amongst the most radical members of Parliament, who, with Whitbread and other ultra-radicals, were strong supporters of Princess Caroline.

In 1816 Princess Charlotte married Prince Leopold, a member of one of the lesser German families, but a handsome and intelligent young man who seems to have been very popular when he settled with his bride in England. The princess soon became pregnant. She was young and healthy, the marriage was popular and she seemed to be becoming distanced from the worst Hanoverian excesses. Royalists and constitutionalists must have felt relief that the succession was acceptably assured. In the event, however, the young princess died giving birth to a still-born son, leaving no one of her generation to succeed after the remaining sons of George III had died.

The death of Princess Charlotte was seen as a national tragedy. Even Byron, convinced republican, wrote elegiac lines:

> Those who weep not for kings shall weep for thee.
>
> Of sackcloth was thy wedding garment made;
> Thy bridal fruit was ashes; in the dust
> The fair-haired daughter of the Isles is laid,
> The love of millions . . .

Shelley, in a pamphlet, *An Address to the People on the Death of Princess Charlotte*, seized the occasion to attack the government and to highlight the death sentences passed on the leaders of the Pentridge rising. The abortive rising, three of whose leaders were publicly hanged after their capture, had been instigated by a government agent and fuelled by the desperation of the weavers and labourers in the bleak climate of post-war Britain. Shelley saw in the savagery of their punishment and the corruption of their trial before a packed jury the end of British liberty.

> Mourn, then, people of England. Clothe yourselves in solemn black. Let the bells be tolled. Think of mortality and change. Shroud yourselves in solitude and the gloom of sacred sorrow. Spare no symbol of universal grief. Weep – mourn – lament. Fill the great City – fill the boundless fields with lamentation and the echo of groans. A beautiful Princess is dead: she who should have been the Queen of her beloved nation and whose posterity should have ruled it forever . . . She was amiable and would have become wise, but she was young, and in the flower of youth the despoiler came. LIBERTY is dead.
> If One has died who was like her that should have ruled over this land, like Liberty, young, innocent and lovely, know that the power through which that one perished was God, and that it was a private grief. But man has murdered Liberty . . .

The image of the death of a hope of renewal and cleansing of the monarchy which Shelley combined with the death of constitutional liberty has a strong resonance. The great display of national mourning for the dead princess went beyond the simple tragedy of the death of a young woman, and helps to explain the remarkable movement which swept the country two years later in support of her mother, the Princess – for a brief time Queen – Caroline. The nation, stirred by the patriotism of the French wars and of Britain's rapidly expanding status as a world power was, perhaps at some level deeper than

The most desolate woman in the world!

Thy daughter, *then,* could hear thee weep ;
But now she sleeps the dreamless sleep.

Phillips's Lament.

ALTERATION.

Near a million of debts gone,
        all gone were her charms—
What! an Epicure have *his own* wife
        in his arms?
She was not to his *taste*—
        what car'd *he* for the ' form,'
' To love and to cherish'
        could not mean reform :
' To love' meant, of course, nothing else
        but neglect ;—
' To cherish' to leave her,
        and shew disrespect

*The deserted queen – one of Cruikshank's illustrations to a rhymed account
of the Caroline affair published in 1820.*

straightforward politics, seeking a symbolic head who could command more respect than the soiled and shabby image presented by the sons of George III.

The Queen Caroline agitation has puzzled historians. One of the most widespread movements of the nineteenth century, it took the form of passionate support for one or other of the participants in a squalid domestic row between characters devoid of integrity or charisma. The explosion of feeling and action occurred in 1820 when the death of George III brought the Regent to the throne as George IV. The new monarch was determined that his wife should not share the throne, and a series of financial and social arrangements was entered into between them by which her title would be agreed, but her presence in England would be avoided. The single issue on which agreement proved impossible was the king's refusal to allow the queen's name to be included among those for whom prayers were asked in the Anglican liturgy. On this apparently minor point all negotiations broke down, the queen returned to England from voluntary exile in Europe, and the government started proceedings in the House of Lords to strip her of her titles and to allow the king his divorce. The story has been told in many places and its significance discussed. It affects the life and reign of Queen Victoria, barely a year old at the time, both as part of the background to her succession and as a key to some of the attitudes and expectations of the British people towards the crown.

Among the effusions which welcomed Queen Caroline's landing in 1820 was a complimentary ode written by a nineteen-year-old Cambridge undergraduate, Thomas Babington Macaulay. The first and last stanzas give a good indication of the tone of the whole campaign.

> Let mirth in every visage shine,
> And glow in every soul.
> Bring forth, bring forth, the oldest wine,
> And crown the largest bowl.
> Bear to her home, while banners fly,
> From each resounding steeple,
> And rockets sparkle in the sky,
> The Daughter of the People.
> E'en here, for one triumphant day,

Let want and woe be dumb,
And bonfires blaze and schoolboys play
Thank Heaven, our Queen is come!

Though tyrant hatred still denies
Each right that fits thy station,
To thee a people's love supplies
A nobler coronation:
A coronation all unknown
To Europe's royal vermin:
For England's heart shall be thy throne,
And purity thine ermine;
Thy proclamation our applause,
Applause denied to some;
Thy crown our love; thy shield our laws,
Thank Heaven, our Queen is come.

Macaulay, though young, was no political innocent, still less so was his father, also a strong supporter of the queen's cause. When the Bill of Pains and Penalties, which would have given the king his way, failed to gain a significant majority in the House of Lords and was withdrawn, Macaulay wrote to his father,

> All here is ecstasy. 'Thank God, the country is saved,' were my first words when I caught a glimpse of the papers of Friday night. 'Thank God the country is saved' is written on every face and echoed by every voice . . .

The sense that failure of the attempt by a morally corrupt king to override the law of the country and the institution of marriage had somehow saved important elements of British life was widespread. Throughout the country the rejoicing at the verdict took the same tone – reluctant conservative clergy were forced to allow church bells to peal out, windows were illuminated – or if unilluminated smashed, not only in radical factory districts like Ashton-under-Lyne but even in Miss Mitford's Berkshire hamlet, where a retired publican, 'a substantial person with a comely wife',

> introduced into our peaceful vicinage the rebellious innovation of an illumination on the Queen's acquittal. Remonstrance and persuasion were in vain; he talked of liberty and broken windows – so we all lighted up. Oh! how he shone that night with candles and laurel and white bows and gold paper, and a transparency (originally designed

for a pocket handkerchief) with a flaming portrait of her Majesty, hatted and feathered in red ochre.

Politically, all this is hard to decode. Some radicals undoubtedly piled into the agitation to gain access to the streets after the Peterloo massacre barely a year earlier. On that occasion a peaceful demonstration for parliamentary reform had been attacked and cut down by the Yeomanry Cavalry and twelve people had been killed. Ministers of the government had congratulated the yeomanry, and radical reformers withdrew from organizing large public demonstrations for some time, for fear of similar attacks. A 'loyal' demonstration in support of the legitimate Queen of England may well have seemed to the radicals to be a target which the military would hesitate to attack. Republicans such as Richard Carlile may have been using the campaign cynically as a means of attacking the crown and the church. Carlile was, as he said 'as careless about the whole system of monarchy as it was possible for a man to be', and as a non-Christian serving a sentence for blasphemous libel at the time could hardly have been very affected by the exclusion of the queen's name from the liturgy. Nevertheless he supported her enthusiastically in his journal, *The Republican*, describing her as 'a virtuous and true heroine'.

Support for the queen went far beyond the bounds of Whig politics or radical protest. In so far as the demonstrations divided on class lines, it was the lower orders who supported the queen and the higher the king. Although Macaulay may have seen rejoicing on every Cambridge face at the queen's victory, a demonstration in celebration by the townspeople was attacked by a mob of eight hundred undergraduates chanting 'King, King, King'. The gifts and messages of support for the queen came from artisans and craftsmen in the manufacturing districts – a watch from Coventry, a carpet from Kidderminster and many more.

But one of the most novel things about the demonstrations of support was the high level of participation by women. The queen was seen as a victim, not only of 'tyrant hatred' in Macaulay's phrase, but of male tyranny. At least seventeen female petitions of support were sent, including one with 17,652 signatures from the 'married ladies of the metropolis'. Some others came from small towns,

THE CRADLE HYMN.

New Version.

ELEVENTH EDITION.

Hush! GREAT BABE! lie still and slumber,
Troops of Lancers guard thy bed,
Chinese gimcracks, without number,
Nicely dangle o'er thy head.

The Qu—n's return's a trifling matter,
Let her face us if she dare;
We will shake our GREEN BAG at her,
She will ne'er be crown'd, I swear.

You shan't fail for want of backing,
What are *Notes* and *Protocols?*
We shall send the jade a' packing,
You shall have some PARIS DOLLS.

Should the GREEN BAG project fail us,
Call in holy WILB—F—CE;
Cant and blarney may avail us,
To accomplish the Divorce.

Start not at the rabble's shouting,
Trust to me and CASTLE——GH,
Never mind old ELD—N's doubting,
Send the saucy jade away.

Never heed BURDETT or HOBHOUSE,
LAMBTON, BENNETT, WOOD, or COKE;
I will flam the dirty-job-house,
CANNING please it with a joke.

Pamper all your Royal fancies,
Order mantles, stays and wigs;
VAN will manage the finances,
HUME may run his idle rigs.

Whether view'd in robes of state, or
Glitt'ring in a fancy dress,
Wisdom cannot make you greater,
Folly cannot make you less.

PARIS DOLLS will much amuse you
When fatigued with forms of state,
Should the living fair refuse you,
They might yield no common treat.

Troops of soldiers shall attend you
Muff'd and lac'd, and gilt so fine,
They shall valiantly defend you,
From the two-legg'd rabble swine.

Hold the PRESS in close submission,
Keep the RADICALS in awe;
Call REFORM the worst SEDITION,
Yet, observe the FORMS of LAW!

Then you'll pass your time securely,
And your baubles all retain;
I shall aspirate demurely
Heavens! what a GLORIOUS *Reign!*

PRICE ONE SHILLING.

"THE DEVIL's BALL; or, THERE NEVER WERE SUCH TIMES."

With some Humorous Poetry, and a coloured Engraving, 1s.

AND A VARIETY OF NEW CARICATURES, BY THE MOST ESTEEMED ARTISTS.

Published by T. DOLBY, 299, Strand, and 34, Wardour Street, Soho.

One of the thousands of coloured prints issued and sold during the Caroline agitation.

though the largest seem to have come from districts like Lancashire, the West Riding and Nottingham, in which a growing radical movement had already demonstrated a considerable presence of women. This does seem, however, to have been the first emergence of a specifically feminine line in popular politics and the support offered was almost invariably to 'a woman wronged'.

The British crown and the British national image have always been strongly associated with female figures. England did better under queens, and there were some among Caroline's supporters who pointed out that her right to the throne rested not only on her marriage but also on her own direct descent from George II. Perhaps the support which the queen evoked was partly from a population which wanted a figurehead rather than an active politician on the throne, and a figurehead in whom the accepted virtues of marriage, fidelity and parenthood would be combined with a benevolent but uncommitted and disinterested role as head of state. Queen Caroline undoubtedly benefited from the popularity of her daughter as well as from the unpopularity of her husband. After the near-hysteria of the celebration of her acquittal, however, she sank into the background, and the pathetic farce of the coronation in which the doors of the cathedral were barred against her aroused little public protest. She died soon afterwards, and her funeral was the occasion of another major demonstration by the London artisans who successfully re-routed her cortege through the city.

It may be that a very strong element in the whole Caroline affair was the assertion by the crowd of the belief that the British monarch, unlike 'Europe's royal vermin', was not above the law or above the customs and institutions of the country. Both George IV and, in a rather different way, his successor William IV had openly flouted the marriage laws and customs of their country. William, as Duke of Clarence, had lived most of his life in conjugal felicity with his common-law wife, by whom he had ten children. He joined the race to produce an heir after the death of Princess Charlotte, and since he seemed to have no difficulty in producing children by his first or second marriages, the nation and the royal family anticipated a continuation of the royal line from him. Whether William's rather boring personality and his unpopularity during the reform crisis of

1830–32 would have been forgotten if he had produced an heir, or whether such an heir would have been inhibited in achieving acceptance by the hangover from the older Hanoverians, was never put to the test. Neither of William's infant daughters survived, and by the time she was about twelve and her uncle succeeded to the throne, Victoria was his almost certain successor. Charlotte and Caroline were still very much alive in the memory of most of her subjects, and must certainly have affected her reception in many quarters. The Duke of Buckingham and Chandos suggested that at the time of Victoria's accession 'the bitter disappointment caused by the untimely fate of the last female heiress presumptive gave deeper feelings to the interest with which she was regarded'. Lady Wharncliffe expressed herself 'delighted with our little future Queen . . . I look to her to save us from Democracy, for it is impossible that she should not be popular when she is older and more seen.'

The two decades before Victoria's succession had seen a variety of popular responses to the monarchy in Britain. By the late thirties there was a polarization between strong Tory and conservative support for the House of Hanover and a more volatile popular feeling which had twice shown itself as a strong attachment to a royal female, combined with at best an ambivalent attitude towards the male Hanoverians.

2

THE THRONE OF ENGLAND

AMONG the changes in the manner of life of the royal family which took place during Victoria's reign, none is more striking than the change in sexual, marital and family behaviour generally. There is no need to believe all the tales of extravagantly immoral behaviour which surrounded Victoria's 'wicked uncles' as she called them, since the fully documented examples provide evidence enough that most of them did not consider themselves bound by those rules of conduct which governed the behaviour of most of their subjects.

Historians of the royal family in this period have been in the main of two kinds. There are a number of books and pamphlets about the Hanoverian kings and princes which detail their crimes and misdeeds, usually without great regard for the distinction between the provable and the unproven. Modern academic and other respectable accounts have tended to fall over backwards to deny or to apologize for their subjects' behaviour, and to allow distance to lend an aura of eccentricity and quaintness to acts which were and remain repulsive to civilized taste. The fact is that George IV, William IV and Victoria's father, the Duke of Kent, were bigamists, adulterers, squanderers of public funds as well as unashamed spongers on friends and subjects, and men who abused their considerable power over others quite outrageously. There may be much in their upbringing and in the very status which they inherited which should make for some charity in judging them. Their sister, Princess Augusta, recalled seeing her two eldest brothers held by their arms and flogged like dogs with a long whip. Cruel discipline as children and young men, followed by the freedom to philander allowed by the Royal Marriage Act may

help to explain their behaviour, but an understanding of the obloquy
in which they were held by so many of their subjects is necessary for
an understanding of the atmosphere in which the young Victoria
came to the throne.

Victoria's father, the Duke of Kent, has had a rather better press
than some of his brothers. His self-indulgence was less flagrant, and
his long-standing relationship with Mme de St Laurent, whom he
abandoned to join the rush to produce a royal heir, had been
childless and relatively discreet. He was, however, in his chosen
career as a military commander, extremely cruel and indeed sadistic.
A recent biographer has spoken euphemistically of the duke's forced
retirement from his command 'on a charge of disciplinary fanaticism
amounting to brutality'. One might reasonably ask whether 'amounting to brutality' is a strong enough term to describe punishments
meted out to serving soldiers of 400, 500 or 700 lashes with a cat o'
nine tails on the bare flesh or of 999 lashes (the maximum allowed) of
an offender in the duke's presence – the deliberate beating to death of
the soldier concerned. These atrocities were inflicted not in time of
war for cowardice or desertion, but on military stations far from any
scene of action for small thefts or infringements of regulations about
dress or deportment. Nor were they and the many other examples in
his career simply illustrative of the harsher military discipline of the
day. The duke's behaviour as commander produced mutinies among
the officers and men serving under him, and led to his formal
removal from his command. A lesser figure might perhaps have been
prosecuted for such misuse of authority, but the royal duke received
only the loss of active command and promotion to the rank of Field
Marshall.

Seeking for an acceptable bride who could be expected to produce
a royal heir, the Duke of Kent settled on the Dowager Princess of
Leinigen. In 1816 the princess was a handsome young widow with
two young children, Charles and Feodora, by her first marriage. She
was a member of the Saxe-Coburg family and her two brothers were
also to be closely connected with the British throne, the one, Prince
Leopold, as husband of the unfortunate Princess Charlotte, and later
as friend and adviser to his niece when she came to the throne, and
the other as father of Prince Albert, who was to be Victoria's

much-loved husband. The marriage of the duke to the dowager princess took place in 1817 and in May 1819, their only child, Alexandrina Victoria, was born. Eight months later the duke fell another royal victim to the appalling medical and nursing practices of the time and died of pneumonia.

Had she been a more obvious candidate for the succession at her birth, Victoria's early upbringing might have been very different. At the time, however, it seemed highly probable that the Duke of Clarence, later William IV, would have children who would be in the direct line of succession, so her childhood was spent largely in the care of her mother. It was a quiet childhood in which the figures of her mother, her governess and her much-loved older half-sister played the most important roles. Feodora, the duchess's elder daughter, was twelve years Victoria's senior. In 1828 she married a German prince and went to live in his country, depriving the little princess of her closest and dearest companion. They continued to keep in touch through correspondence and visits until Feodora's death in 1872. It appears that Victoria found relations with her mother difficult until towards the end of the duchess's life, and her greatest affection was reserved for her half-sister and for her German governess, Baroness Lehzen.

Victoria's mother, the Duchess of Kent, has been far less sympathetically treated by historians than the wicked uncles. No doubt the duchess was a difficult woman, taking bad advice and never really understanding her adopted country. Nevertheless her two daughters were women of great character and ability whose qualities and careers must have owed something at least to their mother's decisions about their upbringing – just as, indeed, Victoria's robust constitution probably owed something to the fact, unusual in royal circles, that her mother breast-fed her.

Had the Duke of Kent lived, disgruntled, always in debt, mistrusted by contemporaries and continually at odds with his brothers, his daughter's position as possible and then probable heir to the throne would undoubtedly have been exploited to a far greater extent than it was. The main male influence in her early life was her uncle Leopold, who was later to become King of the Belgians, but during Victoria's childhood was her educator and adviser. He was a man of principle, liberal in outlook and rightly suspicious of the Hanoverian uncles' behaviour and politics.

Next in line to the throne after Victoria was the most unpopular of her uncles. Many of the rumours surrounding his name may be discounted, but it is necessary to be aware of some of them at least in order to understand the extent to which his presence in 1837 affected popular attitudes towards the young queen.

Ernest Augustus, Duke of Cumberland, was the fifth son of George III. He was a soldier who had fought in the wars in Europe during the 1790s, holding high commands in the English and Hanoverian armies. He acquitted himself well on the field, receiving in action a facial wound which deprived him of the sight of one eye and left him badly disfigured. He seems to have been one of the more intelligent of the princes and to have differed from his brothers in a number of ways, including his adhesion to a strict and moderate diet which made him physically fitter and longer-lived than the others. His commitment to politics was greater than that of the other princes and was pursued with more determination. Unfortunately the politics to which he was committed were those of the most ultra-high Toryism and fanatical Protestantism which embarrassed politicians of all parties. In addition to his unpopular politics his private life included elements and episodes which surrounded him with an aura of evil and of mystery. There can be no doubt that he was innocent of some of the sins of which he was accused, which included that of fathering the illegitimate child of one of his sisters, but in other matters the evidence is strongly against him.

There were plenty of reasons for the Duke of Cumberland's particular unpopularity. Officers in his regiment had protested publicly against the harshness and cruelty of his treatment of men and of junior officers. In 1815 he had married the Princess of Solms, described in a rhyme by Peter Pindar as

> A tender dame of thirty-four –
> Two husbands she had wed before.

She was in fact several years older, and as well as having been twice married, had jilted the duke's brother, the Duke of Cambridge, in between her marriages. She was widely rumoured to have murdered her second husband in order to marry Cumberland, and all in all represented a suitably sinister and unprincipled partner for her unpopular husband. She was never received at Court, and the House of Commons took the almost unprecedented course of refusing an addition to the duke's grant on his marriage, with the result that he spent sixteen years living abroad until he returned to England in time to support the ultra-Tory opposition to the 1831 Reform Bill.

But Cumberland had left England in 1813 amid rumours even more sinister than those with which his wife was associated. In 1811 a scandal had broken when his valet, James Sellis, was found in the duke's chambers with his throat cut. In spite of the findings of a coroner's jury whose foreman was the radical Francis Place, that

Victoria and her cousin George, son of the Duke of Cumberland. The Duke's murdered valet, Sellis, forbids the betrothal (c. 1830).

Sellis had attacked the duke and then cut his own throat, the public
and many nearer to the court believed that Ernest Augustus had
committed the crime and had done so to cover up greater crimes to
which the valet was privy. There is no space here to examine the
evidence, but the fact that the duke's guilt was widely believed was
undoubtedly among the reasons for his unpopularity. Another
reason was the unaccountable influence he appeared to wield over his
brother George. In his earlier years the Prince Regent had had Whig
sympathies, but by the time he came to the throne he had become a
high Tory. Many people seem to have attributed this change to the
Duke of Cumberland's influence. The historian of the royal princes,
Roger Fulford, considered that the influence could not have been
based on love or respect. He quotes George IV saying of his brother
to the Duke of Wellington, 'There was never a father well with his
son, or husband with his wife, or lover with his mistress or a friend
with his friend, that he did not try to make mischief between them.'

The total nastiness of the Duke of Cumberland heightened the
suspicions of those around him as well as of many among the wider
public that his influence in politics and on the throne was exercised
by underhand means. As George's reign neared its inevitable end,
and as it became clear his next brother would not produce an heir,
there was considerable concern about the succession. Victoria was a
child, and little girls in those days were subject to many health risks.
Ernest Augustus appeared a likely possibility as future king. Among
his staff was Major Charles Jones, an officer who had served in the
Peninsular wars and had been wounded. Unwillingly he had been
drafted to serve as equerry to the duke, and indeed the duke stood as
proxy godfather to his only son, Ernest Charles Jones the future
Chartist leader. Among Major Jones's papers is the draft of a letter to
his old commander the Duke of Wellington, undated but clearly
written towards the end of George IV's reign.

> Sir, as first minister for a great nation your attention has no doubt
> been drawn to a consideration of the eventual succession to the throne
> of these realms . . . I will in consequence relate to your grace my own
> as well as every other Englishman's sensations who feels for the
> honour and welfare of his country. I premise that in the course of
> nature . . . our present sovereign will probably ere long pay that debt

to which we are all subject – his successor, should he survive is the Duke of Clarence who it is known has a constitution entirely broken. Then there is an infant which at this moment I believe the country can only look on as a sufficient stop to the claim of the Duke of Cumberland to mount the throne of these kingdoms. Contemplate, sir, the probable removal of that infant, and think of the consequences that might result from the steps to the throne being cleared for that

OLD GRIFFINHOOF.

'Tis most *Ernest*-ly wished that this noted brigand,
Should be no longer permitted to *Cumber the land*.

THE KING OF THE OGRES.
Fee, Fa, Fum!
I smell the blood of freedom,
Let her be alive, or let her be dead,
I'll smash her bones to make me bread!

Radical and many comic journals, including Cleave's *and* Punch *used characters from pantomime and fairy tales to caricature political figures. Here the Duke of Cumberland is depicted as Old Griffinhoof and the king of the giants from* Jack the Giant Killer.

Personage – would the country for one moment indice the idea? do
you not know sir of the midnight murder at St James', of the many
and detestable acts of Moral Turpitude of which that individual is
openly accused? could such an individual from whom all persons
shrink as from the Torpedo's touch be suffered to sit upon the throne
of England? God forbid it – my country I am sure will.

No doubt many such letters were sent to those in authority. This one
has been given at length, since it came from a man who had spent some
years in the duke's service and who was neither a crank nor a radical.
In later letters to his wife he refers to the misdeeds of Cumberland and
to his own knowledge of them. His ambivalence about revealing his
knowledge may be simply explained by the need to retain the goodwill
of his former employers in seeking patronage for his son, who certainly was received by his godfather when the latter visited London in
the 1830s after he had settled into his later role of King of Hanover.

Britain was one of the few countries in Europe whose royal
succession was not governed by the Salic law – the law by which only
male heirs could inherit the throne. Under British law a woman
could succeed to the throne on the same terms as a man under certain
conditions. Victoria took precedence over her uncles and over their
sons, although a younger son in her own family would have taken
precedence. Until her accession the kingdoms of Hanover and
Britain had been ruled by the same monarchs, but the Hanoverian
throne was ruled by the Salic law, and when Victoria came to the
throne of Britain, her uncle Ernest Augustus became King of
Hanover, as the next male in line. In the longer historical perspec-
tive, this was almost certainly a factor which contributed to the
security of the British crown, since the King of Hanover came under
considerable pressure in 1848 and his successor was removed from
the throne by the Emperor of Prussia in 1866. In 1837, however,
Ernest Augustus made no secret of the fact that he considered
himself to be the rightful heir to the British throne as well as the
Hanoverian. His presence on the sidelines was seen as threatening
not only by his political opponents. There was certainly support for
him among his old companions, the ultra-Tories, and Prince Albert
suspected that he or his supporters were behind the assassination
attempts on Victoria which took place in the 1840s.

In considering therefore the atmosphere in which the young queen took up her position it has to be remembered that her succession was not unchallenged, although the challenges, illegal as they were under British law, were necessarily muted. If, as Charles Bradlaugh, the republican writer, later maintained, the young queen was hissed as she drove in Green Park on the day of William IV's death, it was as likely to have been supporters of King Ernest I of Hanover as republican opponents of monarchy who were responsible.

Victoria's accession occurred when she had just reached an age at which a regency was not required. Had William IV died a few years earlier, the problems of appointing a regent who would be acceptable to statesmen and to the public might have been insuperable. As it was, she was remarkably free from apparent royal influences, a fact which must almost certainly have been in her favour with the majority of her subjects. Nevertheless, she embarked on her new role at a very difficult time. An anonymous pamphleteer in the year of her coronation warned her,

> Royalty has never before been exposed to so severe a trial. Yes, madam, the monarchical principle is exposed to a new and rude trial of its strength in your person.

The writer, who may have been Lord Brougham, went on to say,

> It is your fate to have the experiment tried in your person how far a monarchy can stand secure in the nineteenth century, when all the powers of the executive government are intrusted to a woman, and that woman a child.

In retrospect both her youth and her sex can be seen as having been great advantages. By contrast with her predecessors and her immediate successor she appeared less threatening and more malleable to politicians, less vicious and more decorative to the wider public. She was unencumbered by baggage left from her uncles or her father – at least in a public or political sense. As *Bell's Weekly Messenger*, a most loyal and supportive journal, pointed out in a fulsome welcome,

> The greater part of our present generation had never seen a young sovereign of this empire; the last three kings, two of them most completely Englishmen and justly and universally beloved, were known to us only in their declining life, not to say their old age.

The story of the young queen's accession and of her first meeting with her ministers has often been told and was romanticized in the ultra-royal ambience of the last years of the century. At the time, however, neither the security of her position nor the loyalty of her subjects was as firm as was later suggested. The famous picture of the queen's first meeting with her ministers by Sir David Wilkie shows her, young, radiant in a dress of gleaming white, surrounded by a group of benign but rather elderly gentlemen, most of whom are clearly recognizable as the Whig ministers. In fact, the people present on the occasion were not the same as those in the painting, the queen was not wearing white but, quite properly so soon after her uncle's death, a rather dreary black dress. The diarist, Greville, whose account of the occasion is usually quoted, was impressed by the young queen's dignity, grace and charm. She brought to her office, he wrote, 'a decorum and propriety beyond her years and . . . sedateness and dignity, the want of which was so conspicuous in her uncle'.

This impression, however, was gained in the privacy of the council chamber. When she drove to St James's Palace the next morning, Greville was surprised to see 'so few hats off as she went by'.

> I rode down the Park and saw her appear at the window when she was proclaimed . . . The Queen was surrounded by her ministers and curtsied repeatedly to the people, who did not, however, hurrah till Lord Lansdown gave them the signal from the window.

This kind of evidence is difficult to interpret at a distance. The London crowd may have been alienated or uncertain for a number of reasons. The queen was undoubtedly associated by those in the know with the Whig/Liberal politics of her uncle, the King of the Belgians. In an often-quoted letter written some months before the death of William IV, he offered her clear political advice:

> I shall to-day enter on the subject of what is to be done when the King ceases to live. The moment you get official communication of it, you will entrust Lord Melbourne with the office of retaining the present Administration as your Ministers. You will do this in that honest and kind way which is quite your own, and say some kind things on the subject. The fact is that the present Ministers are those who will serve you personally with the greatest *sincerity* and, I trust, attachment. For

them, as well as for the Liberals at large, you are the *only* Sovereign that offers them *des chances d'existence et de durée*. With the exception of the Duke of Sussex, there is no *one* in the family that offers them anything like what they can reasonably hope from you, and your immediate successor with the mustaches is enough to frighten them into the most violent attachment for you.

Her association with the Whigs who were in power at her accession may have annoyed Tory supporters and also perhaps the many members of the London crowd who belonged to the radical groupings which were soon to coalesce in the Chartist movement. However unenthusiastic the radicals may have been, however, they would certainly have feared her 'immediate successor with the mustaches' – Ernest Augustus – more than they feared a Whig-oriented queen.

Because in her later years Victoria became the particular darling of the party, the initial Tory hostility has been forgotten or suppressed. Sir Charles Napier, Commander of the Northern Division of the army during the early years of Chartism, recorded in his diary an account of a dinner given by the magistrates of Nottinghamshire in September 1839.

> Our dinner was a *black* affair. I would not have gone if I had not first ascertained . . . that Lord Scarborough, the Whig lord lieutenant of the county was to go, and so concluded that it could not be a party dinner: yet it was so. The first toast *Church and State*, made it clear we were a Tory party, for the acclamations were immense . . . The next toast was *the Queen*. Glasses were filled, but not a sound of applause followed. Her Majesty's health was drunk in significant silence. No man cried 'God bless her', except myself. Then came *the Queen Dowager and the rest of the royal family*: instantly the room shook with shouts of applause.

Colonel Napier took care to emphasize the loyalty felt by the troops to the new queen when he replied to his own toast. His radicalism and that of his brother never included republicanism, but to many radicals who did hope for a republic, the immediate threat posed by the supporters of the claims of Ernest Augustus to the liberty of the subject and the development of democratic institutions was seen as greater than any posed by the accession of a new young monarch. If the throne was under threat in the late thirties it was from the supporters of alternative male candidates favouring more authoritarian and reactionary policies rather than from republicans.

Modern readers may find it difficult to believe that Conservatives, in our time the supporters of the 'legitimate' succession, could have supported a candidate for the throne who did not have a clear legal title, but, as Bagehot pointed out in his examination of the constitutional place of the monarchy later in the century, it was only in the reign of Victoria that the myth of a direct and unquestionable line of royal succession returned to British constitutional thought. The claims of the Hanoverians rested on suitability and support for the Protestant church rather than on unquestioned legitimacy. It would have been perfectly possible theoretically for the young queen to have been replaced by an alternative candidate without any revolutionary implications for the constitutional status of the monarchy.

Victoria, however, survived the challenge from the Hanoverians and from the undoubted prejudice that existed in some quarters against a female monarch. In popular memory, prejudice may well

The queen of hearts and the knave of clubs.

have been in favour of queens, although only historians would have been familiar with the enthusiasm and hope which had greeted the arrival in London of another young queen, more than three centuries earlier. The sense of relief at the arrival of a fresh and youthful figure after many years of squalid and contentious politics does, however, echo the feelings with which the citizens of London welcomed the young Queen Elizabeth in her pre-coronation entry in January 1559:

> For all men hope in thee, that all vertues shall reyne,
> For all men hope that thou, none errour wilt support,
> For all men hope that thou wilt trueth restore agayne,
> And mend that is amisse, to all good mennes comfort.

Whether this enthusiasm could have been seen as a victory for the feminine principle in politics, or even for feminism itself, has not often been discussed, since the issue was not presented in that form. An interesting comment a century later, however, came from H.G. Wells. He recalled that his mother, who had been born in 1822, was throughout her life a great admirer of the queen – to such an extent indeed that she produced a republican reaction in her son. He described his mother's early years at a small private school:

> An interesting thing about this school of Miss Riley's which was in so many respects a very antiquated eighteenth century school, was the strong flavour of early feminism it left in her mind. I do not think it is on record anywhere, but it is plain to me from what I have heard my mother say that among schoolmistresses and such like women there was a stir of emancipation associated with the claim, ultimately successful, of the Princess Victoria . . . to succeed King William IV. There was a movement against that young lady based on her sex and this had provoked in reaction a wave of feminine partisanship throughout the country. It picked up reinforcement from an earlier trouble between George IV and Queen Caroline.

By modern standards Victoria's coronation was modest, almost casual. Although it was grander than the 'half-crownation' of William IV, so-called because of its cut-price image compared with the grand display put on by George IV, the cost of the event and the celebrations connected with it were considerably less than those of George IV, or of all subsequent coronations. *Figaro in London*, the predecessor of *Punch*, called it 'the shabby coronation' and depicted the queen being carried in a wooden chair by two footmen, a parasol

THE SHABBY CORONATION.

in one hand, the orb and sceptre in the other, with the crown hung
negligently on the back of the chair.

The mood with which the London crowd received the event is far
from clear, although there was the usual loyal turnout for a royal
show. *Cleave's London Satirist and Gazette of Variety* published, as
did most journals, an account of the ceremony and a full-page
drawing of the procession to the Abbey, commenting that it had been
'attended with all that costly splendour by which poor John Bull is so
easily dazzled and delighted'. The following week, however, the
same journal published a 'morning after' cartoon, a complaint about
the cost and 'a few reflections upon the utility and costliness of such
an affair'. The ambivalence shown by *Cleave's* typifies the radical
reaction. In November 1837 it had published a cartoon showing the
young queen setting up a new shop. John Bull and Daniel O'Connell
– the Irish leader – are seen inspecting the goods on sale which

include boxes labelled *CIVIL LIST REFORM* and *JUSTICE FOR IRELAND*. The journal apologized editorially for seeming to depart from its 'comparatively stern and republican nature' so far as to welcome the accession of 'a young, lovely, accomplished and generous-hearted girl to the British throne', justifying its attitude by chivalry and the 'Queenophobia' to be found elsewhere. After the coronation, however, the journal's attitude became increasingly critical and cynical.

In the months before the young queen's coronation her public appearances had been designed to emphasize her distance from her uncles. She rode regularly in the Park between two Whig ministers, never with her uncles or cousins. Her Englishness was highlighted – she appeared in dresses of London manufacture on public occasions and the fact was mentioned in press reports. It seems indeed rather surprising to read that in the November of the year in which her royal uncle had died, she attended a London city banquet in a dress made of Spitalfields silk 'of pink satin . . . the surface covered with silver in the closest embroidery, leaving only lozenge-shaped spaces in pink, in each of which is a full-blown rose with its leaves and buds in silver'. For her coronation, however, as radical journals were not slow to remark, she wore a dress of French silk and lace.

Victoria's advisers before and immediately after her coronation were Whig politicians, chiefly Lord Melbourne, and it was her connection with the Whigs which caused the two most controversial episodes in which she was involved before her marriage.

The first of these, the scandal of her treatment of Lady Flora Hastings, was probably only of concern to the court and its observers and followers in London. It involved an ill-natured response by the young queen to the illness of one of her mother's ladies-in-waiting, when she attributed sexual misbehaviour to a woman who was in fact dying of an unpleasant and painful disease. The unfortunate Lady Flora, whose figure was swollen by the effects of the cancer from which she was dying, was assumed by the queen to have become pregnant through a secret liaison, and was subjected to the indignity of medical examinations as well as becoming the subject of snide gossip and innuendo. The episode increased the suspicions already felt by some of the great Tory families, since Lady Flora's politics were of that complexion, that the queen was too much under Whig influence. It may also, in the gossip of the metropolis, have given an unpleasant picture of the abuse of power and lack of sensitivity in the royal household. Its political importance, however, was far less than that of the other episode, the question of the bedchamber ladies.

The ladies-in-waiting who had been appointed to serve Victoria on her accession were for the most part from the great Whig families. In the small world of early nineteenth-century political intrigue and patronage, the women played a significant part, and the politics of the queen's attendants were considered important. In 1839 Melbourne resigned as Prime Minister when his majority in the House of Commons fell to a mere five. He advised the queen to send for the Tory leader, the Duke of Wellington, to form a government. The Duke, pleading age and deafness, advised her to summon Sir Robert Peel. Peel was the rising star of the Tory party, but at this time certainly did not make a favourable impression on Victoria. When he asked her to make changes in her household, to dismiss at least some of her Whig ladies and replace them with Tories, she refused. She maintained (rightly) that many of her ladies also had Tory connections, and also that their appointment was as her personal attendants and not as political advisers. The issue was to a degree obscured by the political situation in which it occurred. Peel was being asked to form a government without the certainty of a majority in the House of Commons, and a confrontation with the young queen at such a time would have been inconclusive and confusing. He withdrew, and Melbourne continued in office for another two years. When the issue arose again the queen was married and the de-politicization of the household had begun. A few changes sufficed; by the end of her reign only the token change of the Mistress of the Robes was made when there was a change of government, and today no such change is made.

The incident of the bedchamber ladies has gone into the history books as one of the last occasions in which the crown intervened in a political appointment. In fact there were a number of occasions during her reign when her personal attitude to particular ministers or other politicians influenced the actions of governments, for she certainly did not see the crown as being above politics in the modern sense.

3

VICTORIA AND ALBERT

THE next milestone in the story of Victoria's reign was the royal marriage. Because of the non-observance of the Salic law, the Queen of England ruled in her own right. The search for a royal husband for Victoria therefore posed peculiar problems. Any prince who married her would have to accept the role of consort to the sovereign, a role for which there were few models or precedents.

There were a few possible candidates among the queen's royal cousins, including her two contemporaries in the English branch of the family. Her cousin 'George Cambridge', who was eventually to marry a commoner and to be the Chief of Staff for most of his long lifetime, was a possibility, and so was the other George, son and heir of the Duke of Cumberland, now Ernest I of Hanover. This young man, who was eventually to succeed to the throne of Hanover and to be deposed in 1866, had gone blind as a child. In spite of popular cartoons and the claims of Cambridge's biographer, there seems to have been no serious question of either George's marrying the young queen. Her German cousins were much more acceptable and in fact she already, at the time of her accession, had an informal engagement to her mother's nephew, her younger Coburg cousin, Albert. Other foreign royalties were for a time considered, and *Cleave's* joined other low-class journals in speculating on the outcome :

> Of the high-blooded beggars, who e'er she'll prefer
> Though the best is not over-enticing
> Be he German or Dutch, a Von or a Herr,
> John Bull will pay dear for the splicing.

Figaro in London printed a cartoon which showed the queen holding

THE QUEEN'S LOVERS

one of a series of tiny male dolls up to a large crown and complaining, 'They're all too small, NONE of them will fit the CROWN.' *The Times*, in those days of a rather oddly radical Tory persuasion, hoped that the queen would ensure that her consort was of impeccably Protestant background and belief, and in making such her choice, would marry some one of 'comparative weakness and insignificance', credentials which the house of Saxe-Coburg apparently possessed. Although Victoria did have a few second thoughts on the subject, it was her cousin Albert whom she eventually married.

In the matter of her marriage, the queen and the throne were again very fortunate. Of all the possible candidates Albert does appear to have been by far the most suitable, although this could hardly have been predicted in 1839. His father and his elder brother were womanizers and wasters, but he was serious, intelligent and above all committed to the career which he undertook. Although he died comparatively young, he was strong and energetic. He was very handsome and Victoria was passionately in love with him. He himself showed a great capacity for concern and affection for his wife and children – indeed the image of the happy nuclear family which is so important a part of the monarchy in these years owes at least as much to the prince as to the queen. As was to be expected, there were plenty of occasions on which Albert's nationality made him unpopular. He was suspected of alien loyalties and was not universally thanked for introducing a number of German customs into the court and the country. Nevertheless, he was intelligent and undoubtedly serious about science and technology and about art and music. He took a close interest in all affairs of state, acting as the queen's adviser and helping to keep her informed and concerned about every aspect of the affairs of the kingdom.

The royal wedding took place in an atmosphere of sharpening social antagonisms. There was more turbulence in the years between 1839 and 1842 than at any other period in the century. Although the Chartist movement which was the chief expression of the tensions in the country was not primarily republican, there were many suspicions of royal extravagance and of the importation of reactionary ideas of legitimism and absolutism from continental Europe. Xenophobia and fear of Catholic influence were perhaps strongest among the middle classes and the non-political crowd, but Chartists and radicals were not above exploiting these prejudices when protesting against the expenses of a royal wedding and of a foreign prince and his entourage. In one radical cartoon John Bull appears as a jackass, groaning under the weight of bag upon bag of taxes. The Chancellor of the Exchequer eases the load by removing one bag marked *POSTAGE* – the penny post, the world's first cheap prepaid postal system, was introduced at this time – while Lord Melbourne evens things up by replacing it with another bulging sack labelled *QUEEN'S MARRIAGE*. Alongside is another cartoon showing

SATURDAY, JANUARY 18, 1840.

Taking One Burden off the Ass, and Putting on Another.

Shutting Up the Sausage Shop.

Cartoons commenting on the royal wedding.

Prince Albert putting up the shutters of his Coburg Sausage Shop ready to set sail and make a better living 'skinning' the English. Broadsides galore repeated the jibes about Germans, sausages and Albert who

> comes to take, 'for better or worse'
> England's fat queen and England's fatter purse.

These are the comments to be found in the frivolous and theatrical radical sheets, however. The Chartist press was concerned with grimmer matters. In November 1839 there was a rising in South Wales which took the form of an armed attack on a military detachment quartered in the town of Newport. The attack was beaten off by the military and the leaders of the outbreak arrested. The three most prominent, John Frost, William Jones and Zephenia Williams, were found guilty of high treason and sentenced to death by hanging, drawing and quartering a month before the date set for the queen's wedding. In the weeks immediately before the wedding, the kingdom was agitated from north to south by a campaign of support for the Welsh leaders, of petitioning for their pardon, threats of rescue and plans for future risings. 'If Frost is unfairly dealt with,' declared one radical journal 'no Crown in Europe will be worth one year's purchase.' Many petitions were sent directly to the queen, while others made specific reference to her coming marriage in a plea for clemency for the Chartist leaders.

The controversial questions of the prince's status and income which had to be settled before the wedding were therefore discussed against a background of tension and popular disaffection centred around the Newport events. Melbourne may have been a sweet fatherly old gentleman in his role as the queen's political mentor; in his attitude to the discontented poor, whether the agricultural workers protesting against starvation wages in 1834 or South Wales miners and iron-workers in revolt in 1839, he was ice-cold and remorseless. His atti-tude compares unfavourably even with the degree of concern shown by Peel and Disraeli. He was not prepared to make any concession to the recommendation to mercy which accompanied the jury's verdict of guilty on the Welsh leaders. Only the strong recommendation of the Lord Chief Justice who had presided at the trial seems to have influ-enced his decision to commute the sentences. The enormous cam-paign of petitions, meetings and addresses to the queen probably had in the end very little effect on the final decision to commute the death sentences to terms of transportation for life.

This was not, however, apparent to the petitioners, and many working people believed that the young queen had been responsible for the commutation. One street ballad welcoming her marriage offered a song, to be sung to the air 'The Roast Beef of Old England', containing the lines

> Blessings attend her for the pardon she gave,
> The scepter of mercy she extended to save
> The Chartist, from death and an untimely grave,
> Did the mercyfull Queen of Old England
> Old England's Virtuous Queen.

Later, some civic celebrations of the wedding in Wales were interrupted by appeals for the outright pardon of the Welsh

Chartist leaders, but this was not achieved for another sixteen years.

Melbourne may have paid little regard to popular protest and to non-electors in general, but in dealing with the question of the status of the queen's husband and the financial provision to be made for him, he had to face not only the public fear of increased taxation, but the hostility, in the Houses of Parliament, of both high Tories and ultra-radicals. The parliamentary divisions on the question of the prince's money (the Prince's Provision) show some very odd combinations. The government proposed an allowance for Albert of £50,000 a year. This was the sum which had been granted to Prince Leopold on his marriage to Princess Charlotte, most of which he was still receiving. Joseph Hume, Philosophical Radical, proposed instead an annual allowance of £21,000. This was negatived by a large majority, but an amendment by Colonel Sibthorp, the archetypal ultra-Tory backbencher, proposing an allowance of £30,000 was carried by a large majority. The majority included most Tories, a few Whigs and the ultra-Tories and ultra-radicals. It was a considerable defeat for Melbourne, and an indication that the new monarchy was going to be held closely accountable to Parliament in financial matters. Prince Albert may have felt – rightly – that the diminution of his allowance was a deliberate slight. It is, however, true that the amount he received was as much as the total revenue of the whole of his father's territories.

The negotiations about Albert's allowance and his titles and status were carried on in circumstances in which Melbourne found himself frustrated at every point. He wrote to King Leopold,

> This match does not come off at quite a good moment. The times are somewhat unpropitious. Party spirit runs high, commerce suffers, the working classes are much distressed. Your Majesty well knows how the feelings of nations, which have the power of manifesting public opinion, are affected by these circumstances.

The question of the prince's allowance settled, the next problem was his status and title. For these there was no precise precedent. Victoria wanted Albert to be designated 'King Consort' and to share the throne equally with her. Whether in the event she would have accepted an absolute equality of status is doubtful, but it was anyway never put to the test. The suggestion that he should be made a British

The Queen's Consort, 'or the Queen Consort.---Which?

A PROSPECTION OF THREE WEEKS AFTER MARRIAGE.

Pray, Madam, am I not your lawful husband?

Well, sir—then am I not your lord and *master?* Query, sir.—It cannot be disputed, madam, and I say again that I WILL have a considerable increase to my income. What's a paltry £50,000 per annum, for a prince of my importance—that will hardly pay for my amusements. *I will* have another palace, too, and a couple of hunting villas to boot—and more than that, madam, I will interfere in the affairs of the state, and have considerable influence in the army also—and all in defiance of either you or old Jack Bull.

What would be the status of the queen's husband? This cartoon was published in Cleave's *shortly before the royal wedding.*

peer of the realm was also discarded – there were a number of problems involved in such an idea. As a member of the House of Lords he might appear to be interfering too actively in British politics, and in any case a peerage, even a British peerage, was a lesser title than that of Prince, even if Albert was a 'serene highness' rather than a 'royal highness'. Strange as it now seems, although Albert was referred to as the prince consort, the title was not formally bestowed upon him until 1857. After his marriage and his naturalization as a British subject, he received the title His Royal Highness, by which he was always referred to and addressed, but to the end he remained her majesty's husband. In this he differed from his cousin Ferdinand, who, as consort to the queen regnant of Portugal, rapidly assumed the dominant role in their partnership.

The street balladeers produced loyal sheets welcoming the queen's marriage, or scurrilous ones alluding to the prince's poverty and his addiction to sausages. But even the most loyal found some things puzzling.

> Since the Queen did herself for a husband 'propose',
> The ladies will all do the same, I suppose;
> Their days of subserviency now will be past,
> For all will 'speak first' as they always did last!
> Since the Queen has no equal, 'obey' none she need,
> So of course at the altar from such vow she's freed;
> And the women will all follow suit, so they say –
> 'Love, honour', they'll promise, but never – 'obey'.
>> Our cups to the dregs in a health let us drain
>> And wish them a long and a prosperous reign;
>> Like good loyal subjects, in loud chorus sing
>> Victoria's wedding, with Albert her king!

A number of other areas of uncertainty surrounded the royal nuptials. For one thing, was Albert a thoroughgoing Protestant? The fear that Albert, whose stepmother and some other members of his family were Catholics, might be insufficiently committed to the defence of the faith worried some of his future subjects. Among radicals, however, fanatical Protestantism probably seemed a greater threat than Catholicism at that particular time. In 1835 a scandal had arisen when it was revealed that the Duke of Cumberland, a member of the royal family and in direct line of succession to the throne, was

Grand Master of the Orange Order – a semi-secret association of ultra-Protestants which had originated in Ireland in the 1790s. The order and its high-class supporters had been in opposition to the government ten years earlier at the time of the granting of Catholic emancipation, and it had been rumoured that members of the Orange Order were involved in a plot to put the Duke of Cumberland in power as regent in the event of his brother's death. A Select Committee had investigated the order and in 1836 dissolved it. It may well be that Albert's pure Protestant qualifications were marginally improved in the public view by his family association with Catholicism rather than otherwise.

Throughout the reign, Albert and Victoria managed to avoid the extreme anti-Catholicism associated with the early Hanoverians. Although there were anti-Catholic episodes in the second half of the century, and the development of a public education system dominated by the Anglican and Protestant dissenting churches reinforced and extended popular prejudice against Catholics, the royal family was on the whole not associated with fanatical Protestantism. Victoria seemed at times to have some sympathy for the view of her mentor Lord Melbourne, who is reported to have complained that 'things are coming to a pretty pass when religion is allowed to invade private life'. The queen and Prince Albert always observed the forms of Protestant, Anglican worship, and the queen on her accession made the royal declaration against the Catholic doctrines of transubstantiation, the mass and the adoration of saints. Nevertheless, Daniel O'Connell, Irish nationalist leader and Catholic, had no problem in reconciling his politics to the idea of the retention of a common loyalty to the crown after the repeal of the union between Britain and Ireland.

The hostility of Cumberland and the uncertainty regarding Albert's status brought to the fore the vexed question of precedence. The queen wished her husband to rank next to her, but the royal dukes would have none of it and asserted their own priority. Before the undignified procedure of a parliamentary argument had to be faced, however, it was discovered that the sovereign had the right to declare the order of precedence she desired by the issue of letters patent. Albert was therefore promoted above the wicked uncles in

Trying it on.

Albert.—Av, I tink I look vere well in it. It just fits me—ha, ha. I now look ike a King; Victoria, mine tear, vat you tink?

Vic.—Oh! Albert, you must'nt touch that! Pray place it where you found it directly—it's not included in our marriage articles for you to wear, that. It belongs o me only!

Albert.—Well, mine lub, I no dispute it; but you know also, mine tuck, dat vat is yours is mine, now ve *are* married; and so I tink I shall take to vear it as o'ten as I like!

Vic.—Well, now, that CROWNS all !!

public order of precedence, although there were a number of occasions in the first few years of the reign when a certain amount of undignified shoving and elbowing was required to ensure that the correct order was observed.

If the stabilization of the monarchy owes a great deal to the circumstances of Queen Victoria's accession and to her personality, it also owes a very great deal to the personality and the behaviour of her husband. He was in many ways a quite exceptional character to find among the royal personages of Europe. He was able, conscientious, moderately religious, a devoted family man, a good administrator and a competent behind-the-scenes operator. In the early years of the reign when the queen was very much occupied with producing children, his support and guidance became absolutely essential to her. He was from the first better able to work with Peel than she had been, and when the inevitable government change came in 1841 the queen found little difficulty in accepting the new political leadership.

Although Victoria had come to the throne very much 'the queen of the Whigs', her political preferences moved towards the Tories as her reign proceeded. She never seems to have liked the trappings of the traditionalists any more than she liked the high church end of the Church of England. From her childhood she had disliked the bishops 'with their *wigs* and aprons', and was always more at home with simpler forms of worship. She disliked the Tractarians, and respected Newman for going over to Roman Catholicism rather than trying to expand the high church element in the Church of England.

As to the social divisions within the country, she clearly had no doubts about the propriety of class divisions in society and of her own and her family's ordained place in the hierarchy; nevertheless, neither she nor Albert had much sympathy with what they called 'the Foxhunters' – the exclusive circles of the county landed aristocracy. The Belgian scientist Quetelet, who was for a time Prince Albert's tutor, recalled that the prince had once told him that if he were a sovereign he would despise etiquette and live with the most cultivated and intelligent people of the country. When Quetelet visited him in England, he asked if the prince had been able to carry out his intention, to which Albert replied, 'Not altogether.' Nevertheless, the court of Victoria and Albert was more serious and perhaps less aristocratic than those in most parts of Europe. Lord Esher wrote of the queen, in his 1907 edition of her letters, that

> she had strong monarchical views and dynastic sympathies, but she had no aristocratic preferences; at the same time she had no democratic principles, but believed in the due subordination of classes.

These attitudes made it possible for men like Peel and Disraeli, with no pretensions in the way of birth or family, to be accepted not only as ministers but as friends in a way which would have been totally impossible had Ernest Augustus been on the throne. In a famous statement, Lord Salisbury once said, 'I have always felt that when I knew what the Queen thought, I knew pretty certainly what views her subjects would take, and especially the middle class of her subjects.'

On the face of it there could hardly have been a greater distance between individuals than existed between Victoria and her middle-class subjects, especially the women among them. Nevertheless there remains an impression of a middle-of-the-road ambience about the Victorian court. Neither the extremes of high church ritualism nor low church temperance and sabbatarianism found favour there. Taste in music and painting was not avant-garde, but contemporary artists and performers were encouraged. The theatre flourished within parameters of middle-brow taste. New kinds of people received royal honours – the queen was proud of having made the first Jewish peer for example – and little attempt was made to separate the aristocracies of blood and money. An atmosphere of middle-class family virtue surrounded the throne, to such an extent indeed that it has sometimes obscured the reality of royal life and experience.

The turbulent years of the forties were followed by a period of stability and expansion. Most historians are agreed in seeing the third quarter of the nineteenth century as a period of industrial and commercial expansion and of political peace and consolidation. The political challenge of Chartism died away and was replaced by no serious radical presence. The Corn Laws were repealed and British agriculture did not collapse; factory reform was introduced and British industry still led the world. In the manufacturing districts family firms consolidated, in many cases finding good reasons for making space for trade unions of their skilled workers. Cooperative Societies, Building and Friendly Societies provided regularly-employed workmen with possibilities of security which their fathers had signally lacked. Philanthropic industrialists bestowed parks and recreation grounds on their native cities. Britain was becoming the workshop of the world; optimism was possible even outside the ranks of the increasingly prosperous middle class.

The era was ushered in by the Great Exhibition, brainchild of Prince Albert, which was mounted in Hyde Park in its amazing glass pavilion in 1851. Queen Victoria, accompanied by the royal children dressed up in kilts and sporrans, opened the exhibition and rejoiced in the loyal applause from the huge crowd which she saw as being for Albert rather than for herself.

By the time of the Great Exhibition the royal couple had produced seven of their nine children. If there was a consistent burden of anti-royal sentiment throughout the century it was connected with the rapid expansion of the royal family and the expense involved for the taxpayers. The refrain which appeared as a lullaby to the infant Victoria, the first-born, was repeated many times in one form or another:

> O slumber my darling
> While I sing thee a sermon.
> Thy mother's a Guelph
> And thy father's a German.
> The hills and the dales
> And John Bull's money,
> All shall belong
> My dear darling to thee.

Victoria had been born in November 1840, and was followed just under a year later by the male heir Albert Edward, Prince of Wales. Alice Mary Maud appeared in April 1843, Alfred Ernest Albert in August 1844, Helena in May 1846, Louise in March 1848 and Arthur in May 1850. The last two, Leopold and Beatrice, were born in 1853 and 1857. Although she thoroughly disliked the experience of giving birth, as her well-known letters to her daughter show, the queen found some comfort in the introduction of the use of chloroform in childbirth, and her enthusiasm for it helped to spread its use more generally at a time when procreative pain was regarded in many quarters as an essential element in the lives of women.

Victoria had the experience which she shared with most of her women subjects, of constant childbirth as the cost of sex. She was clearly passionate by nature and is reported to have said, when told after the birth of Princess Beatrice that she should have no more babies, 'Oh Doctor, can I have no more fun in bed?' By the middle of

the century, however, the public was being lectured by political econo-
mists on the dangers of over-population. The Chartists were not alone
in pointing to the increase of 'royal tax-eaters' as going against these
teachings. One music-hall song from the late forties reported that

> V unto A so boldly did say
> The State is bewildering about little children,
> And we are increasing; you know we have four,
> We kindly do treat them
> And seldom do beat them,
> So Albert, dear Albert, we'll do it no more.
>   Do it no more!
>   Do it no more!
> No, Albert, dear Albert, we'll do it no more!

If the stereotypical Victorian woman was well-mannered, self-
effacing, demure and devoid of passion, Queen Victoria was so far
from the stereotype as to be almost its opposite. 'A more homely little
body you never beheld when she is at her ease,' the diarist Creevey
had written of her at the beginning of her reign, ' . . . she laughs in
real earnest, opening her mouth as wide as it can go, showing not
very pretty gums . . . she eats quite as heartily as she laughs, I think
I may say she gobbles.'

She retained this habit to the end of her days, and since guests at
the royal table always had their plates removed once the queen's was
empty, and she was served first, there were many complaints,
uttered privately, by hungry diners at the royal table. She began to
put on weight in her teens and was considerably overweight for her
very small frame for the whole of her life. Her first accoucheur
complained of her 'lack of delicacy' and left without

> any very good impressions of her, and with the certainty that she will
> be very ugly and enormously fat. He says that her figure is most
> extraordinary. She goes without stays or anything that keeps her shape
> within bounds, and that she is more like a barrel than anything else.

In spite of all this, however, she lived and retained her faculties until
her ninth decade, and Sir James Reid, who was her private physician
for the last twenty years of her life, recalled that he never saw her in
bed until she was dying. He visited her every morning at 9.30, by
which time she was always up and dressed.

Illustration from A Book of English Song *(1842) with a typical
royal family group. Ironically the wood engraving of the picture
(by H. Warren) was done by the republican W. J. Linton, who was
one of the leading engravers of his time.*

The queen's interest in photography and the usual royal portrait-
painting have left us with a great many images and representations of

Victoria and her family. She seems to have thought it inappropriate for a ruler to be recorded smiling, so that hardly any photographs show her other than intensely serious. People who met her or saw her closely for the first time were often surprised at the mobility and liveliness of her face and manner, and every one remarked on the beauty of her voice. A visitor from France in the late fifties commented on her short upper lip which left her small white teeth exposed. He considered that 'her portraits, by clumsy flatterers, have robbed her of all personality'. Hallam Tennyson recalled that his mother had found the queen to be 'not like her portraits, her face is full of intelligence and very mobile', while Mary Waddington, wife of the French ambassador, noted that she had never seen a smile make so much difference to a face.

The fifties, which saw Victoria and Albert very much concerned with their young family, also saw the Crimean War of 1853–55, and the Indian rising of 1857 which resulted in the transfer of British control in the Indian sub-continent from the East India Company directly to a department of government. Albert maintained close contact with all that was going on and was with the queen when every day she scrutinized the state papers and discussed affairs of state with her ministers. *

Meanwhile the royal children grew up under close and careful parental scrutiny. Albert brought his characteristic seriousness to the matter of the education of the children, and it seems fair to say that sincere efforts were made to broaden and liberalize traditional attitudes towards their education. It is often said that Victoria did not like children, but although she often declared her lack of interest in babies under the age of six months, she showed a close and caring concern for her children, grandchildren and others connected with family and servants. Another departure from the Victorian stereotype seems to have been Albert's close interest in the children in early infancy. When he took his first daughter in his arms the queen commented that he made a better nurse than she did, and she reminded her daughter, after his death, that 'Dear Papa always directed our nursery and I believe that none was ever better'.

Of course, the many demands of her public role and her social programme took the queen and her husband away from the children for long spells. The cosy pictures of the royal parents romping with their young family were not a record of every day or even very frequent occasions. In this, however, the royal family was probably not very different from any wealthy British family in those days of nannies, governesses, nurserymaids and large staffs of indoor servants. There can be no doubt, from the record of journals, diaries and letters, that the royal couple took the care and education of their children very seriously, and that they took great care in the selection of tutors, avoiding the traditional clerics to whom the education of princes had usually been entrusted in past generations. When the queen promoted Prince Leopold's 'instructor' to be his tutor, she wrote to her daughter,

> The only objection I have to him is that he is a clergyman. However, he is enlightened and so free from the usual prejudices of his profession that I feel I must get over my dislike to that.

It was perhaps unfortunate for family harmony that the first child was a girl. The little Princess Victoria had nearly all the virtues. She was pretty, bright and talented. By the age of three she could converse easily in English, French and German, she learnt quickly and was lively and companionable, if at times demonstrating the family traits of wilfulness and temper. She developed a particularly close relationship with her father. By contrast, her brother, less than a year younger, was a totally graceless child. The many attempts made by his parents and tutors to train him up as heir to the throne read as a tragi-comic saga of frustration and misunderstanding.

The relationship between the queen and her son was a crucial element in the story of the monarchy. It helped to feed the republicanism of the 1860s and 1870s and clearly influenced her attitude to later suggestions that she should stand down in favour of a male heir. In Victoria's own perception there seems to have been a continual fear that the monarchy was under threat from democratic and republican ideas, and that a monarch who did not offer an example of probity risked not only his own reputation and position but that of the crown itself. She worried about her son's behaviour and his involvement with circles in which gambling, adultery and worse were part of the ordinary social round. After one case in

which he was involved, the queen wrote in a letter to the Lord
Chancellor,

> In these days . . . the higher classes, in their frivolous, selfish and
> pleasure-seeking lives, do more to increase the spirit of democracy
> than anything else.

Her extreme reaction to her eldest son's lapses was connected also
with her fear that he had inherited the bad blood of the earlier
Hanoverians. Like most Victorians she was a firm believer in
heredity, and is recorded as pointing out that 'there is only my life
between his and the lives of my Wicked Uncles'. Much of the
distrust which the queen felt for her son, however, may go back to
his earliest childhood and the great difference between him and his
elder sister. Greville noted early on that 'the hereditary and unfailing
antipathy of our sovereigns to their heirs apparent seems thus early to
be taking root and the Queen does not much like the child'. Victoria
herself recognized one of the commonest reasons for parent–child
alienation when she wrote with unusual insight to her daughter in
1862, 'Bertie is my caricature. That is the misfortune, and in a man
so much worse.'

The conflict between the generations has been presented in most
histories as the difference between a prudish narrow Victorian court
and a more modern, pleasure-loving and liberal one better suited to
the twentieth century. But it may also be suggested that the court of
Victoria and Albert as well as the more restricted one of the queen's
widowhood was one in which the equality of the sexes was recognized
to a degree, and that the court of Edward VII represented a regression
to the male-dominated era of the early Hanoverians. Edward's consort, Alexandra, a Danish princess with many serious interests, was
humiliated and marginalized by her husband's behaviour. The few
qualities of the monarch – described euphemistically by his sister, who
tried many times to reconcile him to his mother, as amiability and
good humour – were by no means always in evidence, and when they
were it was often in company in which they were exploited.

There is a hint of masculine defence of double standards of sexual
morality in the foreword by Roger Fulton to his book *Royal Dukes,
Queen Victoria's Wicked Uncles*:

When Lord Melbourne told Queen Victoria some of the private history of her uncles, her Diary registered no shock, but after she married Prince Albert in 1840 she completely identified herself with the slightly prudish virtue of her husband's family – the Coburgs – and tried to forget the virile qualities of her father's family.

It is interesting that the contrast between the two eras should be presented in terms of 'virility', and that the change in attitudes during the reign of Victoria should be attributed to Albert's family. Both his father and his elder brother seem to have been womanizers of the regency kind, so that if Albert himself adopted a less 'virile' outlook, it had more to do with personal choice than with family tradition. It is probably the case that Albert during his lifetime and the queen for the rest of the century were unnecessarily distressed by some of the sexual adventures of their sons, particularly the eldest. For all the superficial strictness of sexual morals which the age professed, there was clearly a great deal of 'irregular' behaviour of all kinds, some liberating and some harmless, but a very great deal representing the exploitation of women in a society in which most of the power and most of the wealth was in male hands. To the extent that the values of Victoria's court went against this exploitation and recognized the moral autonomy of women and their authority within the family, a positive contribution was made towards the achievement of equal status for women, even though other aspects of the royal image may have held back the achievement of wider kinds of liberation or of genuine equality.

The lack of accord between Victoria and her heir was certainly not lessened by the fact that the queen was able to establish much better relationships with her daughters than her sons. The problems of the Prince of Wales (always referred to by his childhood name of 'Bertie') are discussed in the letters between the queen and her daughter Victoria when the latter was Crown Princess of Prussia. The Crown Princess retained her childhood affection for her brother, but significantly writes about him as though he were her junior by many years instead of the mere eleven months that separated them.

Queen Victoria was by no means as unsympathetic to 'moral' lapses, whether in sexual relationships or in other forms of personal behaviour, as her reputation might imply. In her eldest son, however, heir to the throne and bearer of the tradition of his saintly father, she could bear no deviation from the strictest canons of behaviour, and she was therefore continually disappointed.

Prince Albert died in 1861, and his death brought to an end one part of the queen's reign. Until his death he had acted as her private secretary, her political adviser and co-director of her family and household. Their mutual affection, and in particular her great affection and admiration for him, made possible a partnership in which her opinion could be guided on many political and other matters by his more serious and knowledgeable approach, to an extent which would have been unlikely and certainly unacceptable had her adviser been a politician or statesman. Albert's influence on questions of policy and of foreign relations may not always have been the best possible, but he took his and his wife's duties very seriously and in general earned the respect of the politicians of both parties. His close concern with political matters could indeed, as the century progressed, have become something of an embarrassment in British political life, and it has been suggested that had he not died young he might have exerted pressure for a more powerful role for the royal head of state in political matters. But he did in fact die at the height of his power and influence, and he left Victoria unexpectedly deprived of an essential part of her life. Disraeli wrote after the prince's funeral,

> We have buried our sovereign. This German prince has governed England for twenty-one years with a wisdom and energy such as none of our kings has ever shown.

A less charitable modern commentator has suggested that Albert, under the guidance of his tutor and mentor Baron Stockmar, had been made into

> a punctual, diligent worker, into a pedantic writer of boring memoranda, into an excellent high official in the Civil Service. But Albert ought to have been educated for a leader . . .

Perhaps these two contrasting views epitomize the contradiction in Albert's position. He himself wrote to Stockmar on the subject,

> Peel cut down my income, Wellington refused me rank, the Royal Family cried out against the foreign interloper, the Whigs in office were inclined to concede me as much space as I could stand upon. The

KING ALBERT SAXE-HUMBUG.   QUEEN VIC.

A German to be Regent raises John Bull's   For young Misses to rule 'twas surely never
    gall,   meant,
But to try on Britain's *Crown* CROWNS all!   But 'tis plain we are now under a MISS-
                                            government.

constitution is silent as to the consort of the Queen; even Blackstone
ignores him; and yet there he was, not to be done without.

Albert's most recent biographer has called him 'perhaps the most
ambitious and astute politician of his age'. His intelligence has been
generally acknowledged, but the idea of ambition is perhaps less
generally considered. He certainly believed that the crown should be
powerful and influential, and it may be that his early death prevented
a constitutional conflict in the later years of the century. The queen
did, of course, exercise a not inconsiderable influence on politics
later in her life, but this was a personal and idiosyncratic one rather
than one based on political principle or even close political understanding. A lady-in-waiting noted in her diary in the 1880s that the
queen had said that

she has always *disliked* politics and does not consider them a woman's
province but that the Prince Consort forced her to take an interest in
them even to her disquiet and that since he died she has tried to keep
up the interest for his sake.

During Albert's lifetime the throne had gained in popularity. The
Queen, preoccupied with a series of pregnancies and royal births,
had nevertheless fulfilled her main public duties, and on those
occasions when she had been unable to be present, her husband had
always been available to stand in for her. She had, indeed, presented
the world with the picture of a female monarch performing her
public and private roles with a degree of grace and dignity which
continued the transformation of the image of monarchy which had
begun at her accession.

Albert's interest in science, technology and the arts is well known.
Victoria's continued patronage owed a good deal to his memory as
well as to her own taste and inclination, and the complex of museums
and institutions in South Kensington which includes the Victoria and
Albert Museum is a legacy of which any reign might have been
proud. Albert left a less public legacy in the form of improved
administration of the royal household and of the private fortune of
the royal family.

The arguments surrounding the prince's allowance and those
concerning the grants to be made to the various royal offspring on
their marriages give the impression that royal finances were entirely
under the control of Parliament. When Victoria was criticized during
the first decade of her widowhood for not fulfilling her public duties
of ceremonial appearances and the entertainment of foreign digni-
taries, some of her critics complained that she was enjoying a civil list
income based on her public activities and was therefore salting away
savings accrued through her withdrawal. In fact in those years she
returned annually part of her civil list income. Nevertheless, as has
been noted, she died a very wealthy woman and her family became
one of the world's richest. In the time of Victoria's predecessor,
William IV, royal finances had been regularized by the surrender of
many ancient rights and of land and estates that were nominally
crown property to the control of the government, in return for an
annual grant of a civil list, divided into the categories of expenditure

on the royal household and the privy purse. The size of these grants is regularly reviewed and revisions have been made over the years in the light of changes in the value of money and of the demands made on the monarch.

Albert's improvements in the running of the royal household probably increased the value of the civil list grant to the royal family. However, there were other sources of royal income which were not surrendered and which were not subject to parliamentary control. One of the most valuable of these was the revenue from the royal duchies. Albert worked hard at reorganizing and increasing these – in particular, in his role of Lord Warden, the revenues from the Duchy of Cornwall. In a recent work, Winslow Ames suggests that by the end of the fifties the royal duchies were producing a substantial income. The prince, he asserts, never received more than about £3,000 a year from his property in Germany, and his annual allowance in Britain of £30,000 did not allow for inordinate extravagance. The capital sum which it is claimed he left to his wife, as well as much of the cost of building the royal residences at Osborne and Sandringham, came from the revenues of the royal duchies, although these projects were also considerably aided by a private bequest to the queen of a quarter of a million pounds in 1852. Since royal wills are not published, there is no clear evidence about the amount of wealth which the Prince Consort left. His official biographer, Sir Theodore Martin, claims that he left no fortune, but an anonymous writer who clearly knew a great deal about the royal household and who wrote in 1898 under the pseudonym 'A member of the Royal Household' claims that he did in fact leave a very substantial capital amount. When he came of age the Prince of Wales, who was also Duke of Cornwall, received the revenues from the Duchy of Cornwall in addition to his annual grant.

Apart from the civil list grants, royal finances were largely screened from public view. Income and other direct taxes did not apply to royal revenues, so that apart from the clearly evident fact that the private wealth of the royal family increased greatly during Victoria's reign, not much can be said with certainty. That some of the expansion and consolidation was due to Albert's careful stewardship and sound business sense, however, seems incontrovertible.

During Albert's lifetime the royal family had acquired, in addition to the state residences of Buckingham Palace and Windsor Castle, an estate in the Highlands of Scotland – Balmoral – and another on the Isle of Wight – Osborne House. Holidays were spent in one or other of these when they were not taken abroad; the state residences were usually reserved for official entertaining. Both Victoria and Albert were enchanted with the Highlands. The establishment at Balmoral of the royal residence helped to create a craze for all things tartan and Scottish. Visitors to the royal residences, especially Balmoral, were startled by the clashing tartans displayed in the domestic furnishings. The royal children appeared in public and in photographs and portraits dressed up in Highland costume – that is, in kilts with plaids and sporrans, frilly shirts and all the nineteenth-century trimmings. One of the most intriguing cameos of the century is the account of Victoria's four-year-old grandson William (later, as Kaiser Wilhelm II, to lead the German forces against Britain in the First World War) at the wedding of his uncle Bertie biting the bare legs of his younger uncles, Arthur and Leopold, as they tried to discipline him.

The fashion for the trimmings of an imaginary Highland culture was part of the dominant romantic ideology of the first half of the nineteenth century. George IV had had himself painted in the full rig-out in 1822, and Victoria enthusiastically followed his lead, lending a spurious royal and aristocratic cachet to tartans, clans and even bagpipes. It was a harmless enough fancy, and was accompanied by a very genuine love of the country and respect for the people. Victoria always preferred cold weather to warm, cool houses to overheated ones. Marie Mallet, her maid of honour for many years, recalled, 'I can safely say I never remember a warm congenial day in the Highlands during the many months I spent there.' For the queen, though, and to some extent for some of the younger members of the family, Balmoral was an enchanted place, far away from the city and the obligations of official life. This particular affection is important for several reasons, among them the loyalty which the crown evoked even from the Gaelic-speaking Highlanders, in contrast to the alienation felt by the Irish, and the strange story of the relationship between the queen and her Highland servant John Brown.

'After the death of the Prince Consort in 1861', as her granddaughter recalled, 'she rarely came up to London.' Without her husband, Victoria took only a very limited part in the public political life of the country for more than a decade. For the first few years of her reign she had headed a bright court in London, attending the theatre, entertaining and taking a lively interest in everything that went on in the capital. After her marriage she allowed herself to be guided and advised in political, administrative and governmental matters by her husband, and in her domestic life concentrated on her family and on the houses which she and Albert bought and built. It is possible to underestimate her active concern in those years – Arthur Ponsonby, for example, pointed out that the selections from her diary, published as *Leaves from a Journal of Our Life in the Highlands from 1848 to 1861*, described domestic matters only.

> It would not require much research, however, to pick out a date recording some colourless, unimportant incident and to find in her correspondence on the same day some letter to the Prime Minister or the Private Secretary expressing in the most vehement language her desire to interfere in high matters of national importance. But this was all excluded from the volumes and the general public, including radicals and even republicans for a short time, were satisfied there could be no harm whatever in a monarch who spent all her days so innocently in her Scottish retreat.

Although she was always involved in public concerns, however, she was guided and supported by her husband, and his death brought about a crisis in her attitude to public matters as well as marital and family concerns. A third period of her life began with his death, one which saw the most active republican movement and the period in which cynicism and suspicion of the crown, which had not been much in evidence since her accession, began to reappear. It was a period in which the public demands upon her as monarch conflicted strongly with her inclinations and her preoccupations, and in which the possibility of the occupation of the throne by a woman again came under question.

By the time the queen had been virtually invisible for half a decade, even loyal monarchists began to complain.

> I know I am very bold, and with all my loyalty I am a little ashamed to

speak so much like a Whitechapel democrat. But what is a true-hearted Englishman to do, when he sees everything going to the bad; a fine business being ruined, as you may say – for I do look upon this 'Throne of England' as a fine little business if properly managed – all going to smash, because there ain't no right head, no 'Governor King'. A woman can't attend to it like a man. There's the Foreign market to visit, and a lot of work to do to keep it all right and square, and it ain't to be expected that a Lady, with a heap of troubles on her mind, and the anxiety of finding suitable husbands for her daughters, can look after the shop as well. So she leaves it all to the Receivers, and a pretty mess they are making of it. My advice is, Ladies and Gentlemen, that that son of hers should put away his 'Bull-terriers' and his betting book; cut the sporting buttons from his coat; try on one of his father's, if it be ever so shabby; give that loud and vulgar scarf-pin to his groom; change those gaiter boots for a pair of decent flexura-elevans; kick out the Receivers; take the trouble from his Mother and give us a respectable, right down undeniable definition of the word 'Throne' according to your humble servant to command

MISTER BROWN
(The Husband of 'Mrs. Brown')

The curious pamphlet from which this extract is taken, called *Brown on the Throne*, was published, with a slight disclaimer, by a respectable publisher in 1871. It was written in mock-demotic language, comparing the throne to a greengrocery business, but strongly urging, in its mock-humorous style, both the unsuitability of a woman for the duties required of a monarch and the threat of people standing not too far away, who considered that they could manage the shop better than the widow-woman who was in nominal charge.

Dissatisfaction with the queen was expressed in various quarters and took more than one form. At its simplest it was a complaint of the queen's invisibility. She retired to her country dwellings after Albert's death and could only be persuaded up to the capital with the greatest of difficulty. To begin with, no one found such behaviour especially remarkable. Victorian widows did retire, and some of the queen's extravagant behaviour and displays of grief were not much more than would have been indulged in by many of her subjects. It was customary, and continued to be so until well into the twentieth century, for widows to wear dark clothes for the rest of their lives if they did not re-marry. Anyone who could afford to do so erected lavish and sentimental memorials and inscribed verses on them. Full mourning – that is dressing in black and wearing a black veil – was often observed within families for anything up to a year after a bereavement, followed by half-mourning, during which grey or lavender could be worn, for a further six months. Many widows never abandoned their black dresses. Black-edged writing paper was used for months or years, while many families of all classes preserved draped pictures or other relics of the dear departed. All this public signalling of private grief seems to have become more formalized and more generally indulged in as the century progressed, and Victoria's extravagant use of all the forms may have encouraged similar behaviour on the part of her subjects, although she certainly did not initiate the customs. However, when it is recalled that as a young queen a quarter of a century earlier, she had appeared in brilliant dresses within a very short time of her uncle's death, the heavy court mourning which followed the death of the Prince Consort may be taken as one of many examples of the great increase in ceremony and ritual which came to surround the throne as Victoria's reign continued.

Public opinion therefore did not necessarily condemn the queen for retiring into widowhood, but there were considerable sections who considered that such retirement, although proper, was not consistent with maintaining the role of a monarch. The queen, they considered, should abdicate in favour of her son, who was, after all, of age at the time of his father's death.

This kind of criticism of the queen was basically a gendered one. It was quite proper for a female to feel unable to take any public role in the absence of a husband, there were plenty of female tasks still remaining for the queen to carry out – arranging weddings, advising her daughters on the care of her grandchildren, perhaps attending the occasional social function in support of her son or in his place. Dowager queens were more common in English history than widowed reigning monarchs, and many people considered that, having provided a male heir, her work was now complete.

Queen Victoria had never had much regard for the intellectual and moral qualities of her eldest son, and the bad relations between them were exacerbated at the time of Prince Albert's death by a scandal involving an actress. The queen believed this had worried Albert at a time when all his strength should have been husbanded to fight his illness. In 1863, at a ceremony of hitherto unparalleled magnificence, the young prince married Princess Alexandra of Denmark, and the London crowd became accustomed to the sight of the prince and his remarkably beautiful bride driving through the capital. Her uncle, King Leopold, reminded the queen of the greater public presence of the Prince and Princess of Wales, knowing that this was one thing that might persuade her to take up some of her own public functions again. For, whatever the general public view on the question, Victoria herself never seems to have contemplated for a moment making way for Bertie to become king. She never trusted him with the smallest item of important or confidential matters of state, and indeed never really seems to have been convinced that he would be able to manage what she considered to be the most important position in the world, that of ruler of Britain. In their correspondence on the matter her daughter used the inadequacies of her brother to persuade her mother to carry on in the immediate aftermath of Albert's death:

> You know, beloved Mama, what would most likely be the fate of the nation if God were to remove you now. In 20 years time all that causes us such alarm with Bertie may be changed and softened. But heaven forbid beloved Papa's work of 20 years should be in vain.

Those of her subjects who sympathized with her withdrawal from public life considered that she should do so properly and hand over her public role to a man. Those who wished her to remain on the throne, or who respected her decision not to abdicate, not unnaturally expected her to fulfil all the demands of her position, after a decent interval of mourning. In a sense, in making this demand they were going against the received wisdom about the proper role of women. For the queen to continue in a public role distinct from that of wife or mother was again to except her from the rules of behaviour by which her subjects were increasingly governed.

Albert died in December 1861, and Victoria made her first public appearance after that event when she drove out in an open carriage on 21 June 1864. During her seclusion rumours about her illness or even madness circulated. As she began to be seen in public again, even though not as frequently as some of her advisers would have liked, these rumours died down, to be replaced as the decade continued by stranger ones concerning her relationship with her serving man, the former Highland ghillie, John Brown.

The John Brown story is an odd one, and one that has caused some embarrassment to historians and biographers. Before looking at some of the questions it raises, however, it should be noted that this is probably the most outstanding example of the different standards applied to the behaviour of men and women. Had Edward VII – or any other king for that matter – been widowed during his reign and sought consolation in a close relationship, whether overtly sexual or not, with a palace servant to whom he gave small gifts and on whose friendship and support he relied rather than on that of his relatives, historians would probably have barely noticed it. In fact, given the vast sums of money and gifts of land, rank and status which past royal mistresses and bastards have received, an episode like that of Victoria's infatuation with John Brown would seem remarkably innocent and simple. For a woman, however, to engage in an irregular sexual relationship, even if it implied no disloyalty to an existing partner, was and is regarded as so outrageous as to be almost unthinkable.

After her husband's death the queen clearly became more self-absorbed and self-centred. She withdrew from many of the public functions of the monarch, and viewed with some ambivalence those which she still fulfilled. In her private and personal life she encountered on a more exalted scale the problems faced by many Victorian 'relicts'.

The loss of her husband was a physical as well as a social and spiritual loss. She wrote in her journal, 'What a dreadful going to bed! What a contrast to that tender lover's love! All alone!' She had always had a strongly passionate nature. In a letter written a few months before Albert's death she had declared,

> My nature is too passionate, my emotions too fervent, and I am a person who has to cling to some one in order to find peace and comfort.

Within less than a year she had lost her mother and her husband, both of whom she considered had placed her at the centre of their universe. No one now remained for whom she took unquestioned first place. Her children were either young and dependent or had already broken away to start their own adult lives, and demanding though she undoubtedly was, she was also honest enough with herself to realize, as a number of references in letters and journals show, that the relationship between parents and children can never be one of equality or complete reciprocity. A second official royal marriage was on the face of it an impossibility. It is hardly surprising that given her situation and her nature, she should seek a close relationship with another adult. What is surprising is not the fact of the John Brown relationship itself, clear and undeniable as it was, but the extent to which she was prepared, for the sake of it, to go against so much of what seemed to be her nature and her beliefs. For the whole John Brown episode deeply offended her children, upset and alienated some of her closest retainers and servants, caused gossip and ribaldry among those of the general public and press who took note of it and clearly worried her court and political advisers. Victoria had a strong sense of public duty and the highest possible regard for the dignity of her office. She was also strongly convinced of the need to observe the class divisions in the society of her time. Nevertheless, the evidence is overwhelming that these considerations did not prevent her from contracting a relationship with a man who was of humble birth and was by occupation a servant, a relationship closer and more intimate than she had with any other man after her husband's death.

4

VICTORIA AND JOHN BROWN

THE elaborate and dramatic mourning, the preservation of mementos, the commissioning of portraits, busts, jewels and volumes in memory of the departed loved one which occupied the queen's time and energy in the months following Albert's death were to be repeated only once again in her lifetime. In 1883, when her servant John Brown died, she mourned his death by keeping his room as he had left it, preserving his gifts and other mementos, commissioning statues and busts which were distributed throughout the royal residences, and treating his memory with more ceremonial than she observed about any other death except that of her husband, even including those of her children who pre-deceased her.

As the years go by, new evidence continues to turn up to reinforce the view that the relationship between the queen and the ex-ghillie was of a different order from that of employer and servant. The fact that the Brown relics and memorials were immediately destroyed by the new monarch after her death itself supports this view, one which was very widely held at the time. Most biographers, however, faced with the evidence, have tended to fall back on the conclusion that a sexual or even a close emotional relationship would have been impossible at that time between two people of such disparate social positions. Perhaps the twentieth-century obsession with actual sexual relationships has led to the overlooking of other unquestioned aspects of the relations between the queen and the ex-ghillie which seem to have been essentially connubial, including the manner in which Brown's death was mourned, and the relics which she ordered to be placed with her in her coffin.

A modern feminist – indeed, perhaps almost any modern woman – faced with the suggestion that the queen took a lover a few years after her husband's death, might well say 'so what?' Young widows re-marry, Victoria was only forty-two, clearly unlikely to make another open and conventional marriage. Although her choice might have distressed members of her family, from the wider view of the constitutional role of the monarchy a liaison with a social inferior who was without political ambition and who made only moderate personal demands on the sovereign was preferable to any liaison with a member of the upper classes or of a foreign royal family, around whom political suspicions would inevitably have clustered. What the whole Brown affair does illustrate is the double standards required of male and female public figures as well as the extent to which the queen was prepared to re-write the rules of conduct and social precedence when it suited her. Historically, one must also ask whether the affair and the rumours and scandal which it evoked ever seriously endangered the throne.

Perhaps the chief reason for reopening the Brown question and for its continuing interest must be the light it throws on Victorian hypocrisy. For all its decadence and corruption, Regency England and its political life had the appeal of an open society free to comment on the practices of the great and the splendid, and to find humour and subjects for moral comment in the human or more than human lapses of the powerful and the mighty. As the nineteenth century progressed, a refinement of taste and of sensibility rejected much of the crudity of earlier ages, at least among respectable society at all levels, but at the same time a proclivity developed to cover up or to deny aspects of human behaviour which did not square with the accepted ideal. In particular sexual behaviour became disguised in attitudes and codes which not only concealed much of the reality of what went on, but restricted and punished certain members of society out of all proportion to any misbehaviour of which they may have been guilty. A few politicians were pilloried and destroyed by the invocation of accepted standards – although those who led the attack were often themselves leading double lives or acting out conventional roles whose hollowness we have only recently begun to understand.

More importantly, perhaps, many people in lower stations were bullied, blackmailed or trapped by the social or legal controls imposed in the name of an ideal code of behaviour. Women above all were constrained by financial dependence and the laws governing the custody and care of children from breaking out of unhappy marriages or entering unsuitable ones. If it could have been shown that the queen, a middle-aged widow of the highest social status, with a young dependent family, had indulged in a sexual liaison with a man who was younger and by a considerable degree her social inferior, a great many cherished taboos and judgements would have been challenged. If some republicans and anti-monarchists used the Brown question to play on existing prudery and prejudice to discredit the queen, others used it as a means of pricking the bubble of false morality – particularly the denial of sexual impulses to respectable women – which informed the dominating public teaching of church and state.

The story of the relationship between the queen and John Brown has already been told in several places. There may well be more to be discovered. Indeed it seems as though about once in every decade new hints arise, new documents are discovered, new deathbed revelations are disclosed and another denial is issued from the Palace. There is no need, however, to go much beyond the already published accounts to realize that the uncontested evidence can bear more than one interpretation. The question would seem to be, was John Brown's relationship to the queen that of a spouse or a servant?

Lady Longford, whose knowledge of the queen and her journals and letters is probably greater than any other historian's, bases her conclusion that the relationship was essentially that of employer and servant on her assessment of Victoria's character. Such an opinion must be respected. Nevertheless, it remains an opinion, and one which seems to go against fairly strong evidence. It is possible to read the story differently, indeed it becomes more possible the further one gets from the Victorian and post-Victorian attitudes to sexual questions, for the half-century between 1890 and 1950 was the period above all in which 'Victorian' attitudes to personal and family morality were at their height. A generation less bound than its predecessors by the image of stern morality presented in the queen's last years may be more prepared to find the history neither shocking nor particularly surprising.

Victoria possessed the ability to justify her own actions to a very high degree. She also regarded the Highland people as differing in many ways from the rest of the British population, so that her promotion of Brown out of the servant class was only a minor exercise in self-deception. She more often referred to him as her 'friend' than her servant, and it seems unlikely that she habitually addressed servants in the tone of the cards cited by Lady Longford herself, one of which was addressed in the queen's hand, 'To my best friend J.B. From his best friend V.R.I.'; another wished 'A happy New Year to my kind friend from his true and devoted one. V.R.I.' Both these date from the late seventies. A letter to John Brown in October 1874 addresses him as 'darling one', hardly an expression which would have been used by an employer to a servant, however favoured, of the opposite sex. What is more, it is clear that the queen was quite capable of re-defining the social status of any of her subjects. In an interesting exchange with her daughter in 1885 about a projected marriage in the latter's family which appeared to cross certain class barriers, the queen described a letter which she had written to the Empress of Prussia in support of the marriage:

> I . . . said morganatic marriages were unknown in England and if a king chose to marry a peasant girl she would be Queen just as much as any princess . . .

More than once later in her life she was to insist on the power of the monarch to raise men of humble status. When she was protecting one of her Indian servants who had been publicly attacked as being of low social origin, she commented that the suggestion was

> really outrageous, and in a country like England quite out of place . . . She has known two archbishops who were the sons respectively of a Butcher and a Grocer, and a Chancellor whose father was a poor sort of Scotch minister. Sir D. Stewart and Lord Mount Stephen both ran about barefoot as children . . .

To insist on the power of the monarch to raise a subject's social status is not, of course, to suggest 'democratic' views. Victoria had insisted on royal matches for her children, even if some of the royalty involved were pretty minor ones, agreeing only to one exception in the case of her daughter Louise, who married a Scottish nobleman. In her later years, however, she expressed concern about the intermarriage which was occurring within the European royal dynasties, giving it, for example, as a reason for opposing the marriage of her son Alfred to the daughter of her cousin George, ex-king of Hanover. As with many other subjects, she expressed contradictory views at different times, but seems to have had no problem in admitting to equality in personal terms a Highlander chosen by a monarch for his perceived virtues. What is more, as well as her general attribution of a special character to Highlanders, she believed that Brown was not of peasant stock, but was descended, if not from the aristocracy, at least from a Scottish gentry family. In 1872 she promoted him to the rank of 'Esquire'. The servant had been remodelled by royal favour – a circumstance by no means unknown in our history.

Throughout her life Victoria was attracted by masculine good looks, and also felt a strong need for male support and admiration. Although it is probably true that, apart from her Albert, those with whom she formed the closest relationships and exchanged most confidences were women – particularly her half-sister and her eldest daughter – she seems always to have needed a sympathetic male presence. Perhaps she needed someone to fill the role of the father she had never known; perhaps the largely feminine environment in which she had grown up gave her an exaggerated respect for men's opinions and enjoyment of their company. Perhaps it was just that Albert had filled such a large part of her life – although even before her marriage her uncle Leopold and Lord Melbourne had been her close advisers. For whatever reason, she was certainly very much a woman of her age in this. Wilful and opinionated as she could be, and passionately defensive of her own view on many questions, she always needed masculine support and confirmation of her actions and decisions. In her letters and journals after her husband's death there is the continual plaint not only of grief and loss, but of loneliness:

> I must work and work, and can't rest and the amount of work which comes upon me is more than I can bear! I, who always hated business, have now nothing but that! Public and private it now falls upon me!

He, my own darling, lightened all and every thing, spared every
trouble and anxiety and now I must labour alone!

John Brown, as has often been pointed out, was already in the royal
service in Albert's lifetime. He was already a favourite among the
Highland servants – who were in any case a favoured group, and
helped to look after the royal family in their most relaxed and familial
environment. A painting by Carl Haag shows Brown attending the
queen and prince and their children at a picnic in the autumn of
1861, and there are many accounts of the participation of the royal
family in a very informal way in 'below stairs' occasions among the
Balmoral servants. Highlanders were regarded as different from the
common run, and there could be nothing very surprising in the
queen's decision to bring one of her Balmoral servitors south to look
after her horses and perform other outdoor functions when she was
reluctantly obliged to leave her Highland retreat. Over the months
and years, however, he moved from being an outdoor servant to an
indoor one, and rapidly then to the role of the queen's constant
personal attendant, taking precedence over all other staff and in
many matters over the royal children. The queen was very often
alone in his company, and rumours in word and in print spoke of a
royal child fathered by Brown, whether or not after some kind of
marriage ceremony.

There may well be more to be revealed about the relationship
between the queen and her friend which will finally settle the
question of its exact nature. To an extent, it matters far less now than
it did a hundred years ago, and it will become more of an antiquarian
curiosity as it retreats into history. The queen inspired loyalty in
those who served her, and lived in an age in which the repetition of
gossip and indiscretions was not as highly rewarded as it has since
become. It was also an age in which almost all jobs depended on
patronage. A high degree of security or alternative sources of
patronage were necessary for anyone without resources who challenged the rich and the powerful in any way. An irregular relationship, even a sexual relationship, between a widowed queen and a
palace servant could be – and was – hinted at or openly asserted in
print, but there was not much financial gain to be had and not a little
might be risked in the way of loss of position or actual prosecution if

the writer went too far. Republicans were poor, gossip was cheap, and there was no vested interest prepared to pay large sums for royal disclosures. Even a child, scandalous though its birth might have been, would have had no serious implications, since there were nine legitimate offspring and two families of legitimate grandchildren already in existence. It was in the general interest of those surrounding the queen to keep anything they knew 'within the family'. Diaries, letters, deathbed reminiscences that have turned up in the hundred-odd years since Brown's death may lend weight to the rather more sensational interpretation of events, but for the most part those closest to the court and best able to judge the evidence have put the dignity of the crown and respect for the memory of the queen first, and have not risked the notoriety which any reopening of the matter must bring. There are, however, plenty of hints in 'official' sources as well as the statements in unofficial ones which have to be considered before making a final judgement.

When John Brown died, the queen, in a letter to her secretary Sir Henry Ponsonby, compared the shock to that of Albert's death:

> The Queen is . . . utterly crushed and her life has again sustained one of those shocks like in '61 when every link has been shaken and torn and at every turn and every moment the loss of the strong arm . . . is most cruelly missed.

The comparison with the death of her husband was accentuated by the similarity in the pattern of mourning followed by the queen, and by her decision to produce as a memorial another volume of extracts from her journal. The first volume, produced in memory of Albert and consisting of extracts from her journal describing excursions, visits and other non-official occasions they had enjoyed together, had been a runaway success when it finally appeared in 1867. Nearly twenty years later the death of John Brown prompted the production of a second selection, this time from the years since Albert's death, dedicated to the memory of John Brown. These were the queen's only two publications in her lifetime. The second volume was dedicated 'gratefully' to 'MY LOYAL HIGHLANDERS, and especially to the memory of my devoted personal attendant and faithful friend JOHN BROWN'.

The picture that seems to emerge from the evidence of the

relationship is of the widowed queen's increasing reliance on Brown in the years immediately after her husband's death. She begins to quote his (extremely mundane) opinions in her letters to her family, and in the Highland journals, as published twenty years later, he appears on nearly every page. She clearly found him physically attractive – he was indeed, to judge by the large number of paintings and photographs which survive, handsome and upright with the fair good looks that the queen admired. Following the pattern of more conventional marriages, infatuation and a strong sexual attachment – for if Brown and the queen were indeed lovers it must have begun some time in the mid-sixties – probably mellowed into companionship. The tone in which he addressed her and she him certainly seems more like that to be found in an affectionate marriage relationship than between mistress and servant.

Anecdotes recorded at the time and later illustrate an astonishing degree of familiarity in Brown's speech and manner towards the queen. It should be remembered that most of those around her, including her sons, stood in great awe of her and always approached her with humility and circumspection. One story told by the barrister John Berry Torr recalls a chance meeting on a Highland road which took place when he was out walking in the Balmoral district. Rounding a corner he saw the royal carriage standing empty at the roadside and the queen standing beside it alone with Brown who was in process of fastening a shawl about her shoulder with a brooch. As he appeared, the queen jerked her head and received a scratch from the pin, exclaiming in 'no measured language', to which Brown replied, 'Hoots, wumman, can ye no hold yer heid still!' Torr was far from being the only observer to comment on the roughness of Brown's manner to his mistress, and the rather homely image invoked is reinforced by another anecdote from Ponsonby, who records that one of the Maids of Honour met Brown on his way to the royal carriage bearing a picnic hamper and asked if this contained the queen's tea. 'Wall, no,' he replied, 'Her Majesty don't much like tea. We tak' out biscuits and sperrits.'

A rather less reliable source was reported by E.E.P. Tisdall, who described a letter which he received after he had placed an advertisement in a national newspaper, asking for anyone with personal or family recollections of the queen and John Brown to write to him. The letter contained a photostat of a note on the queen's paper which had been recovered by a footman from John Brown's wastepaper basket. Since the photostat had gone missing by the time Tisdall wrote his book, there are good reasons for treating the story with caution, nevertheless it carries some conviction. It appears to have been the sort of note that the queen was known to send to members of her household with written instructions, in this case concerned with the arrangements for the allocation of the bathing machine. Amongst the prosaic household details was a single sentence – 'Oh, forgive me if I offend, but you are so dear to me, so adored, that I cannot bear to live without you.' Then followed more detailed arrangements, this time for a visit to 'my Scottish capital' and the ending 'your own loving one' without a signature.

Perhaps more convincing, because very reticently recorded, is the story told by Randall Davidson, later to be a popular and influential Archbishop of Canterbury but in 1883, at the time of John Brown's death, just installed in the prestigious post of Dean of Windsor. Davidson had been chosen by the queen for his qualities of charm and tact and he very quickly became a friend of the queen's private secretary and Keeper of the Privy Purse, Sir Henry Ponsonby. The two faced together the considerable problems of dealing with the queen's reaction to John Brown's death.

Brown died at Easter 1883, after only a few days' illness. The queen was plunged in misery and wrote passionately to his relatives, 'Weep with me for we all have lost the best, the truest heart that ever beat.' She always seems to have taken pleasure in funerals, and perhaps modern thinking now finds this concern rather less grotesque than it was once considered. Public mourning and the open expression of grief were certainly widely indulged in by all classes in the nineteenth century. Even so, the funeral given to Brown might have seemed more suitable for a victorious general or a much-loved senior statesman than a royal servitor. The queen's wreath of myrtle and white blossoms on the coffin carried a card inscribed in her own hand, 'A tribute of loving, grateful, and everlasting friendship and affection from his truest, best and most faithful friend, Victoria R & I.' In time a granite memorial was erected over the grave with a biblical inscription and some especially composed lines by Tennyson, the poet laureate. A life-sized statue of Brown which had been commissioned by the queen and executed by the sculptor Edgar Boehm stood after his death in the garden of the cottage at Balmoral in which the queen had worked in his company while he was alive. Gold brooches and tie-pins bearing his image and the queen's monogram, VR, were distributed among palace servants and court officials, and plaster casts of his bust were distributed throughout the various royal residences.

In the immediate aftermath of Brown's death the queen decided to embark once more on authorship and set about composing a memoir of the former ghillie for publication. She also proposed to publish his private diary. The problem of dissuading the queen from these publications was one of the first faced by the young Dean in his new position. Davidson recalled later that his talks with the queen during his first year at Windsor were of a more intimate nature than any during his years of service. He wrote in his diary, after a conversation on the subject of John Brown,

> Interview with the Queen.
> Most touching, solemn and interesting, but terribly difficult. O God give me guidance and grace, if I am to be called on thus to counsel and strengthen in spiritual things.

He must, it seems, have gained the queen's confidence by his sympathetic discussion with her, for it was in the end his determination, carried to the point of threatened resignation and involving two weeks of banishment from the chapel and the royal presence, which persuaded the queen to abandon the idea of publication of the diaries and memoir, and allowed Ponsonby to burn both. On the anniversary of Albert's death in December when it was the queen's custom to hold a memorial service, Davidson recorded that he was asked to prepare a special prayer for the service, mentioning her favourite son, Arthur, away in India, the deaths that year of two outstanding churchmen, including his predecessor as Dean, 'and above all, J.B., a very difficult task. But it must be done'.

Those closest to the queen were clearly worried about her attachment to Brown. Lord Cairns commented after attending the Balmoral servants' ball,

What a coarse animal that Brown is . . . Of course the ball couldn't go without him . . . Still, I do not conceive it possible that any one could behave so roughly as he does to the queen.

In 1896 Marie Mallet wrote to her husband describing a visit she, as lady-in-waiting, had paid in the queen's company to the church where Brown and other members of his family were buried. They laid wreaths on more than one Brown family grave and

H.M. got out of her chair and laid a bunch of fresh flowers on John Brown's grave with her own hands. The Prince Consort and the Highland tenants share this unique honour. . . . it is really very curious, but do not mention the curious fact.

Lord Carlingford recorded in his journal in 1885 that he was received by the queen at Balmoral, 'in Prince Albert's room as usual', and had a long conversation about suitable verses to be inscribed on a seat erected in memory of her recently-deceased uncle Leopold. She also wanted his opinion on a suitable inscription to be added to Frogmore (the mausoleum in the grounds of Windsor Castle where Albert was buried) 'in memory of my dear faithful friend' (i.e. John Brown). 'This infatuation,' Lord Carlingford wrote, 'is wonderful. It is patently absurd to hear his name pronounced, when one would expect another.' Mary Waddington was invited to visit Frogmore many years later and recorded that it contained a recumbent marble statue of Prince Albert, with room beside him for the eventual addition of the queen, a 'pretty monument' to Princess Alice, who had by then died young, 'with a child in her arms', and a tablet to the memory of John Brown as 'a grateful tribute from Queen Victoria to the faithful servant and friend of 34 years'. Numerous other such references indicate the depth and strength of the queen's attachment.

To some commentators the openness of the queen's affection and dependence was itself a proof of the 'innocence' of the relationship. The fact that the queen herself felt no guilt, however, is not necessarily an indication of the spirituality of the connection. Without in any way suggesting that the queen ought to have felt guilty, it is still possible to suggest that the popular nickname of Mrs Brown may not have been too bad a description of the queen in the two decades between Albert's death and that of John Brown.

It has been suggested that the shouts of 'Mrs Brown!', the fears

expressed by the ministers of violence against the person of Brown if
he did as the queen wished and accompanied her to a military review
in Hyde Park in July 1867, a well as the gossip and innuendo to be
found in some disreputable journals, show that the rumours about
the queen were circulating mainly among the lower orders. As with
the stories about Victoria's wicked uncles half a century earlier, some
historians have dismissed the public expression of these rumours as
the lucubrations of ignorant and illiterate gutter journalists. In fact,
in both cases the rumours can be seen to have started much nearer
their objects. One of the first reports of the 'Brown' stories to appear
in print was in a series 'English Photographs', No. IX in *Tinsley's
Magazine* in October 1868. Under the nom de plume of *An American*,
its author complained:

> Finally I am compelled to reprobate the loose manner in which
> Englishmen think and speak about women. They have a bad habit of
> telling gross stories over their wine, and often sully a reputation by an
> innuendo.
>
> Soon after my arrival in England, at a table where all the company
> were gentlemen by rank or position, there were constant references to
> and jokes about 'Mrs Brown'. Confounding her with Arthur Sketch-
> ley's heroine in *Fun*, I lost the point of all the witty sayings, and
> should have remained in blissful ignorance throughout the dinner had
> not my host kindly informed me that 'Mrs Brown' was an English
> synonym for the Queen.
>
> I have been told that the Queen was not allowed to hold a review in
> Hyde-park because Lord Derby and the Duke of Cambridge objected
> to John Brown's presence; that the Prince of Wales took a special train
> for Osborne to remonstrate with his royal mother when the *Toma-
> hawk*'s 'Brown Study' was published; that the Queen was insane, and
> John Brown was her keeper; that the Queen was a spiritualist and
> John Brown was her medium – in a word, a hundred stories, each
> more absurd than the other, and all vouched for by men of consider-
> able station and authority.

The stories listed here are a hugger-mugger which included some
real incidents; for example, it was indeed the case that the queen fell
out with her ministers on the matter of attending the Hyde Park
review, a more extended confrontation being avoided only by the
cancellation of the review upon receipt of the news of the capture and
execution of the Emperor Maximilian in Mexico. Other parts of the

account are probably untrue. Spiritualism was a great craze at the time, and although it is not impossible that the queen might have shown some interest for a short time, most historians who have examined the evidence have found nothing to support the association of Brown with spiritualism. In fact it seems out of keeping with the character and behaviour of both. The rumour of royal madness had arisen on numerous occasions since the days of George III. It is now generally accepted that his madness was associated with a specific disease, porphyria, which, although it ran in the royal family, was most certainly not inherited by his granddaughter. Victoria herself feared the hereditary taint and her outbursts of temper may sometimes have approached the pathological, but her relationship with Brown was certainly not that of patient and keeper.

But surely something in the tone in which the anonymous author reported the conversation he had witnessed suggests that allegations were being made which were of a more damaging nature than the items he referred to. There is nothing in his list which justifies his suggestion that the references were unchivalrous and gross. He was clearly hinting at more libellous stories not reproduced, stories which associated the queen with her ex-ghillie in an even more intimate way. In a letter to her equerry Lord Charles Fitzroy, the queen had spoken of 'wicked and idle lies about poor, good Brown' which were being spread by 'ill-natured gossip in the higher classes'.

By the late sixties these stories had gone beyond the circles of upper-class gossip. Writing to the Earl of Clarendon in the summer of 1864, Lord Howden privately expressed an opinion which seems to have been widely held. It would have been well, he suggested, 'for her own interest, happiness and *reputation* to have abdicated on the day her son came of age. She would then have left a great name and great repute.'

As it was, gossip was widespread. In September 1866 the *Gazette de Lausanne* in Switzerland reported that the queen had secretly married John Brown and was carrying his child. 'If she was not present for the Volunteers review, and at the inauguration of the monument to Prince Albert it was only in order to hide her pregnancy.' The British minister at Berne lodged a formal complaint against the Lausanne paper, but the story did not die. It certainly did not help to quieten gossip and allay suspicions when the annual exhibition at the Royal Academy which opened in May the following year contained a large portrait by the fashionable painter Sir Edwin Landseer of the queen and John Brown together. The queen sits side-saddle upon an elegant Landseer mount (rather different from the sturdy ponies which appear in photographs taken at the same period) reading a dispatch with papers and dispatch box on the ground below her. True to his style, the artist had portrayed royal dogs gazing with almost human devotion at their royal mistress, but outshining all, at the horse's head, stands John Brown in kilt, sporran and glengarry gazing at her with even greater respect. The queen, it appears, was delighted with the picture and had herself suggested minor amendments before its completion. At her request an engraving was made from it for popular consumption.

At around the same period, the queen commissioned Boehm to produce a bust of John Brown. Catherine Walters, the courtesan better known by her nickname of 'Skittles', who was closely associated with London society in the sixties, later passed on to her friend Wilfred Scawen Blunt something of what Boehm had told her about his adventures during the three months he spent at Balmoral working on the bust. Blunt wrote her story in his diary which has only fairly recently emerged from the fifty years' moratorium that was placed on it at his death. This story is at third hand, was remembered after the event by the teller, and is part of the record of a member of a very gossipy upper-class set. It comes, however, from someone to whom sexual adventures were not shocking, and who might be expected to be the recipient of such a story for that very reason.

Boehm told Skittles that he had seen a great deal of the queen as well as of Brown, his model. The latter he described as a 'rude, unmannerly fellow' whom he had much ado to keep in order during his sittings, but said,

> he had unbounded influence with the Queen whom he treated with little respect, presuming in every way upon his position with her. It was the talk of all the household that he was 'the Queen's stallion'.

Boehm, Skittles maintained, saw enough of Brown's familiarities with the queen to leave him with no doubts of Brown's being allowed 'every conjugal privilege'. Skittles' story was confirmed for Blunt by conversations with Lord Rowton, who had been Disraeli's secretary and had 'represented' his late master at Brown's funeral. Rowton is generally regarded as loyal to the point of sycophancy, so that if he did in fact, as Blunt says, 'attach . . . a sexual importance to her affection for John Brown', Blunt had good reason to take his view seriously.

The discussion about the relationship between Victoria and John Brown has been almost entirely conducted from the point of view of the queen. But Brown's own behaviour is more like that of a husband than a servant, not only in the many examples which are given of his bold way of addressing her, but in his fidelity and constant attention to her from the middle sixties when he became her official attendant. From that time until his death he was her constant companion, and developed no independent relationships of his own. Although he remained in close contact with parents and brothers, and indeed involved the queen in a number of family events, his home and the centre of his life was where the queen was. He had his own servant and comfortable quarters in the royal residences and had the freedom of the royal coverts – to a degree that infuriated the queen's sons and sons-in-law, who objected to taking second place in access to the best shooting. Brown was present at the most private moments between the queen and her children. Because Bertie would not receive him with sufficient respect, the queen almost never visited the home of her son and his wife at Sandringham during Brown's lifetime, devoted though she was to the Princess of Wales.

From all this patronage, John Brown did not seek rank or money, or at least only in a very moderate way. He had a very comfortable billet where his heavy drinking was not held against him, but if he had not also been attached by strong bonds to the queen, he could have married or retired in comfort at almost any time after the first few years. Clearly the relationship was a two-way one, as one small surviving document suggests. The extracts from the queen's journals which remained unburnt at her death make only restrained and straightforward references to Brown, although not in any way concealing her respect and affection. Among the letters which the queen sent to members of Brown's family and which have remained in their possession, however, are one or two which shed a more contemporary light on her feelings. One letter, undated but written to his brother Hugh at the time of John's death, recalls an episode from 1866, when the queen had been very distressed by the sudden death of one of her little grandchildren. She had recorded the conversation in her diary, and copied it for Hugh and the rest of the Brown family:

> Dear John said to me: 'I wish to take care of my dear good mistress till I die. You'll never have an honester servant.' I took and held his dear kind hand and I said I hoped he might long be spared to comfort me and he answered, 'But we all *must* die.' Afterwards my beloved John would say: 'You haven't a more devoted servant than Brown' – and oh! *how* I felt that!
>
> Afterwards so often I told him no one loved him more than I did or had a better friend than me: and he answered 'Nor you – than me. No one loves you more.'

To the end of her life she insisted that two small salt cellars, a gift from Brown, should appear on her luncheon table, and to the end of her life a fresh flower was placed daily on the pillow of his room in Balmoral. A visitor to the royal closet at Windsor saw in the middle of the room a large table bearing a 'forest of framed photographs', among which were a number of portraits of John Brown in various poses.

But perhaps the most interesting evidence comes from the recently published life of the queen's physician, Sir James Reid. Reid was her personal physician for the last twenty years of her life, a serious and dedicated attendant who clearly became an important and trusted member of the royal household. He undertook a number of negotiations requiring tact and diplomacy, and the queen clearly respected his opinion and advice in matters other than just those of the family's health. When the queen died it was Sir James who prepared her body for burial, according to her clear instructions. Mrs Tuck, the queen's serving woman, read to him the instructions 'about what the Queen had ordered her to put in the coffin, some of which none of the family were to see'. These included various items of close sentimental importance – the Prince Consort's dressing gown, a cloak embroidered by Princess Alice, a plaster cast of Albert's hand and numerous family photographs. When these had been covered by a quilted cushion and before the queen's body was laid on top, members of the royal family came to pay their last respects and the Princess of Wales laid some flowers on the small body. The queen was then lifted in to the coffin, and the maids arranged her dressing gown, veil and lace. The 'royalties' then all went out, and Reid's diary continues,

> I packed the sides with bags of charcoal in muslin and put in the Queen's left hand the photo of Brown and his hair in a case (according to her private instructions), which I wrapped in tissue paper and covered with Queen Alexandra's flowers.

The family were then admitted for the final farewells.

To all this must be added the undoubted fact that the queen's children, particularly her eldest son, bitterly resented Brown. When the queen was quite seriously ill, her children were not permitted to see her, but Brown was admitted to her room when he pleased. Sir Henry Ponsonby wrote to his wife,

> You say you wish the Prince had the pluck to say how much he hates JB. He does say so to me, and that, as he is brought into so much prominence at Balmoral is one of the reasons why he hates Balmoral.

The portrait of Brown in full Highland regalia, which had been painted at the queen's request, disappeared after her death and only surfaced again half a century later. When rediscovered, there was a hole through it, as if it had been attacked with a cane or an umbrella. Popular opinion suggested that this might have been the last protest of Edward VII, who speedily cleared the royal residences of that and all other Brown memorabilia.

The new king did not, however, totally exorcise the ghost of John Brown by his house-cleansing. Sir James Reid, who continued to serve as physician-in-ordinary to Edward VII, was summoned by the king in September 1904, to deal with a delicate problem. One of the physicians who served the royal household in the Highlands, Dr Profeit, had died, and his son was asking King Edward for money – amounting in effect to blackmail payment – for a trunk full of letters from Queen Victoria to his father 'about John Brown'. Reid was entrusted by the king with the delicate task of handling the negotiations and was able to hand over to the king the more than 300 letters, many of them 'most compromising'. What their contents were will presumably never be known, since Sir James's green memorandum book in which he made his own notes on them was burnt after his death by his son, and there can be little doubt that Edward, who seems not to have shared his mother's attachment to family documents, would have destroyed the originals.

The evidence strongly suggests that the queen's relations with Brown were those of infatuation and strong sexual attraction, gradually mellowing into an affectionate partnership which strongly resembled a stable marriage. In retrospect it would seem to have been a harmless, indeed rather a touching episode. Although the suspicion and secrecy with which it has been recorded and discussed illustrates the very different standards of sexual behaviour expected from male and female monarchs, Victoria's relations with John Brown were not merely a reversed version of the many affairs and casual sexual relationships indulged in by some of her male predecessors and descendants. Nevertheless, there was no way at the time in which such a relationship could be made acceptable or even understandable to the court or the public. The population as a whole expected the queen to fulfil the duties for which she and her family received enormous sums from the public purse. Politicians feared the growth of republican and anti-monarchical feeling; they also found the problems of keeping the queen informed greatly exacerbated by her insistence on remaining at a distance from the capital. She continued her practice of receiving state papers daily and reading and commenting on them, and even during her period of withdrawal from public and ceremonial functions she retained those of her association with government. Her ministers, therefore, were obliged to transmit documents to Osborne, sometimes to Balmoral, and to maintain regular epistolary communication in place of personal contact. Disraeli pointed out tactfully that 'carrying on the Government of a country six hundred miles from the Metropolis doubles the labour'. Gladstone complained to Lord Rosebery that 'the Queen alone is enough to kill any man'. Mary Ponsonby, radical wife of the queen's private secretary and a member of a family with long political traditions, believed that the authority of the crown might come into question. 'If they don't take care,' she wrote in a letter in 1871, 'Gladstone will show his teeth about Royalty altogether, and I wouldn't answer for its lasting long after that.'

If John Brown filled part of the gap which Albert's death had left, it was as a loving and supportive companion, not as a political adviser. There are stories of his political comments, which included hostility to Gladstone on the grounds of his high church 'half Roman' affiliations rather than his liberalism, but in the main his influence was exercised in household and family matters rather than in political ones. The rumours which began to circulate in the press and among the wider public were directly related to the queen's continued absence from her public duties. The public had become reconciled to having a female monarch, but she must fulfil both the public role and the private female one with dignity and honour if she was to retain their loyalty.

As the loss of Albert receded, the less respectful journals began to suggest that the queen was occupying herself with purely domestic matters in unsuitable company. *Punch*, in July 1866, published a spoof 'Court Circular':

> Balmoral, Tuesday.
>
> Mr John Brown walked on the Slopes. He subsequently partook of a haggis. In the evening, Mr John Brown was pleased to listen to a bagpipe.
> Mr John Brown retired early.

Similar skits appeared in other journals, less openly suggestive than the *Lausanne Gazette*, but more accessible to British readers. The radical and republican press was slow to repeat the gossip, however, concentrating rather on the expense of the monarchy. Whether from fear of official action, or from a desire to keep republican politics free from the accusation of gossiping, the 'Graccus' column in *Reynolds's Newspaper* which regularly advocated republican views, got no nearer to repeating the Brown accusations than the comment, 'We do not care to reproduce in our columns the many extraordinary causes that are assigned for the Queen's seclusion in the pages of our foreign contemporaries.'

But rumours were rife. A new comic journal, *The Tomahawk*, which began publication in 1867, rapidly gained a large circulation

'A Brown Study' from The Tomahawk, *August 1867.*

by exploiting the Brown story. Beginning with a Court circular-like
report of the queen's Highland activities, it followed with a full-page
cartoon 'Where is Britannia?', which showed the throne empty, the
royal robes draped over it (it was the custom, when Parliament was
opened without the queen's presence, for the royal robes to be

draped in her place), the crown insecurely balanced on top and the British lion dozing on the floor. In August 1867 the notorious cartoon 'A Brown Study' showed the throne again, but this time the crown is at the side, under a glass case, and leaning negligently against the throne, pipe in hand and legs crossed, is a dour figure in Highland dress, apparently undisturbed by the British lion which is roaring at him in the foreground.

This cartoon has usually been credited with 'opening up' the John Brown question to the public. The *Tinsley's* article appeared a month later. A pamphlet, in form the same as the many 'part-works' in which popular writers issued novels at that time, was, according to the inscription on the front, 'purchased in the street' in September 1867. Entitled *John Brown or, The Fortunes of a Gillie* and priced at one penny, it promised to be the first of a series, of which further parts would be ready in October. Inside, the few pages that remain in my copy contain a story about a Highland family amongst whom the son John shows early signs of hubris and ambition. The whole cover of the pamphlet is taken up with a cartoon, clearly based on the famous *Tomahawk* one, but differing in a number of points. Here John Brown has his hand firmly on the crown, and is leaning – in the opposite direction from the original – upon it. No objecting British lion is in sight, but instead the Highlander is surrounded by admiring ladies dressed in rich national costumes which include Welsh, Scottish, Spanish, Chinese and several others. Although unmistakably John Brown, the central figure does not have the lowering look of the *Tomahawk* version, but is smiling grimly. Underneath is Dr Johnson's famous dictum, 'The noblest prospect which a Scotchman ever sees is the high road that leads him to England.'

The rumour that the queen and John Brown had been joined in matrimony by some kind of informal marriage ceremony, and that their relationship had resulted in the birth of a son, has persisted. Some historians seem to attribute the story to a small pamphlet by Alexander Robertson, printed (but probably never issued) in 1873. But the story was around long before then. The *Lausanne Gazette* story had been published in 1866, the *Tinsley's* and *Tomahawk* items in 1867. By the time Robertson was repeating apparently widespread Highland gossip in 1873, the infant, if he existed, would have been,

Purchased in the streets 13 Sept 1867 212

JOHN BROWN;
OR,
THE FORTUNES OF A GILLIE.

Part 1 only
6

ONE PENNY WEEKLY.

"The noblest prospect which a Scotchman ever sees is the high road that leads him to England."—DR. JOHNSON.

OSBORNE & ROSCHONE,
16, BEAR ALLEY, AND 29, FARRINGDON STREET, LONDON, E.C.,
AND ALL BOOKSELLERS AND NEWSAGENTS.

☞ PART I., FOR OCTOBER, CONTAINING Nos. 1, 2, 3, & 4, WILL BE READY IN A FEW DAYS. PRICE SIXPENCE.

JOHN BROWN ;

OR,

THE FORTUNES OF A GILLIE.

PART I., FOR OCTOBER,

Ready in a Few Days,

CONTAINS THE FOLLOWING ILLUSTRATIONS:—

No. 1.

JOHN BROWN GIVING AN UNCO' EARLY SPECIMEN OF HIS PROWESS BY
NEARLY STRANGLING HIS BROTHER.

No. 2.

THE OPPORTUNE ARRIVAL OF JOHN BROWN SAVES THE HIGHLAND HOME
FROM DESTRUCTION.

No. 3.

THE QUEEN REVEALS HER REGARD FOR JOHN BROWN, AND EXTORTS AN
OATH FROM THE DUCHESS NOT TO REVEAL IT.

No. 4.

THE QUEEN CAUTIONED AGAINST IMPRISONING JOHN BROWN.

OSBORNE & ROSCHONE,

STEAM-MACHINE

AND

GENERAL PRINTERS,

16, BEAR ALLEY, AND 29, FARRINGLON STREET, LONDON, E.C.

NEWSPAPERS MACHINED.

All descriptions of Letterpress Printing executed with neatness and despatch.

in Robertson's own phrase, 'a thumping Scottish laddie'. Robertson was not particularly concerned with national politics, and it seems very unlikely that his pamphlet, which was nothing more than a printed rehearsal of his private grievances, received, as the historian Tom Cullen has suggested, 'a wide vogue'. Certainly most of the allegations which Cullen found in it are not in the copy I have, and since he does not state the location of the copy he has seen, his interpretation must remain questionable.

In reality, the interesting thing about the Robertson letter is that it calls on stories gathered in his native Highlands not to bolster up a republican case of any kind, but to explain the apparent immunity from ordinary legal process of the family of the Duke of Athole, against whom Robertson had a legal case concerning tolls and a road bridge. 'The Dowager Duchess of Athole,' he maintained, 'has often been heard to say "If they dare meddle with us about these horrid accounts, *I will let the cat out of the bag*."' What exactly 'the cat' was is hinted at by a series of allegations about the presence of J— B— in a certain bedroom on the occasion of royal visits to Dunkeld House and the suggested role of the Duchess as 'howdy' (the Highland term for midwife) in a delivery some nine months later. The child concerned had, it was alleged, been placed with a Protestant pastor in the Swiss canton of Vaud to be brought up.

The point of the story, which is full of hints and information from informants (in some cases named) among 'the people of Dunkeld and those residing near Balmoral', is that as the result of their association. with Brown and the queen, the Athole family enjoyed the support of 'some unconstitutional influence' which was depriving him of his legal rights.

> As I mentioned in my letter of the 11th July, the Athole family profess to be in the knowledge of some great secret, which can be used with such magical effect, that it can not only whitewash them from their delinquencies regarding the missing toll accounts, but enable them to overthrow any ministry, dissolve Parliament, or even abrogate *Magna Carta*.

This is the voice of the mild paranoia that attacks people in every generation who tangle with the British legal system. There always seem to be people whose legal case is apparently watertight and

soundly based but who through some slip-up or subjective judgement fail to gain a verdict. Political influence or extra-constitutional
pressure seems the only explanation. The more simple answer that
the word of a duke will usually carry more weight in court than that
of a small country landowner seems not to meet the case, and
conspiracies or sinister influences have to be sought. The fact that
Robertson found his sinister influences in the gossip about the
relations between the duke and the queen neither invalidates nor
legitimizes the stories. It merely offers the occasion for them to be
recorded. As recently as 1979 when the possibility of new evidence in
support of the story of the affair and the child was again raised, the
Observer asserted that the tradition still lingered in the Balmoral
district.

But even if Queen Victoria was 'married' by some private
ceremony to her erstwhile servant, even if she bore him a child – at
the age of forty-seven or forty-eight by no means in itself impossible
– and if the child was put out to a Protestant pastor in the canton of
Vaud to be brought up, the world was none the worse for these
events. Queen Victoria was not a delicate creature in her youth and
middle age, and the possibility of a lusty relationship with Brown,
with whom she was known to share a taste for whisky and for the
brisk air of the Highlands seems by no means an impossibility. Lord
Clarendon, visiting her at Osborne in January 1869, reported that
'Eliza is roaring well and can do everything she likes and nothing she
doesn't'. She was certainly fond of food, and of Scotch whisky,
which to Gladstone's horror, she added to her claret. In those
'missing' years before her return to a more public role, she may well
have retreated into a more self-indulgent way of living which she
would have found it quite easy to justify.

In these years, she certainly endowed Brown with authority over
her household. Stories abound of the slackness and indiscipline that
resulted from his rule. Lord Carlingford's journal noted that
improvements attempted by Sir John Clayton Cowell, who was
Master of Her Majesty's Household from 1866 to 1894, were much
easier to effect after Brown had gone. '*He* was all powerful – no
servant had a chance of promotion except through him, and he
favoured no man who didn't like his glass.' 'At Balmoral,' Lord John

Manners observed, 'more curious things go on . . . than I should have dreamed of.' The way the household was run was an open scandal, but the queen indulged her favourite above her court and family.

In time the situation came to be accepted, and the more diplomatic among the politicians and courtiers learned how to adapt to Brown's presence and authority. Disraeli addressed him with easy familiarity, and always remembered to mention him in letters to the queen. He once remarked that before any piece of legislation he had to be sure of the agreement of 'the two J.B.s', i.e. Johns Brown and Bull. The whole long Brown episode, however, undoubtedly widened the gulf between the queen and her eldest son.

Brown died quite suddenly at Easter 1883, of erysipelas, a skin inflammation which was at one time known as St Anthony's Fire, and which was probably made more serious by delay in treatment. Sir James Reid attended the dying man, and signed the death certificate of death from erysipelas, but his journal recorded that Brown was also suffering from delirium tremens, and there can be little doubt that his alcoholism was a major contributor to his death, as it was later to kill his younger brother. Heavy drinking was not frowned on at Victoria's court, and one at least of her sons, Prince Alfred, Duke of Coburg, died prematurely largely as the result of his uncontrolled drinking. The queen's toleration of heavy drinking, indeed her own indulgence in whisky, may have owed something to John Brown's influence; Cowell, as Master of the Household, reportedly 'came to blows' with John Brown on the question of the amount of alcohol consumed by the servants, and on this issue as on most others, the queen invariably sided with Brown. It is also clear, however, that the queen did not by any means always take the strait-laced attitude to pleasures of the flesh that has usually been attributed to her.

5

THE REPUBLICAN
ALTERNATIVE
1   1819–1861

VICTORIA has been credited with ensuring the survival of the British monarchy in a century which saw many European thrones tumble. By the end of the nineteenth century the throne was firmly established as part of the British system of government, and it has survived into an age in which universal suffrage, decolonization and the end of the nation's status as a major world power might well have encouraged the development of republicanism. Before going on to look at the last twenty-five years of her reign – the years in which the consolidation of the monarchy was definitively achieved – it is worth considering whether a serious republican alternative to the monarchy was put forward at any time during her reign.

Some of the reasons usually suggested for the stabilization of the British monarchy during Victoria's reign are based on very dubious accounts of the history. She was very far from being politically neutral or from keeping the crown above party politics. Although she was, perhaps, more 'British' in style than the earlier Hanoverians, German was the language mainly spoken in her family circle, many of her closest family connections and loyalties were with other parts of Europe and there were indeed murmurs at many points against her friendship for and support of discredited foreign royalty. She has often been described as 'middle-class' and has been credited with establishing the popularity of the monarchy with that important and expanding section of the population. There is some validity in this argument, since Victoria and her husband certainly rejected the extremes of frivolity and self-indulgence which had characterized the upper classes of an earlier age. In doing so they did indeed encourage

PRINCE ALBERT "AT HOME."
WHEN HE WILL SUSTAIN (NO END OF) DIFFERENT CHARACTERS.

Punch *being heavily sarcastic about the number of public offices and honours the prince accepted, especially the Chancellorship of the University of Cambridge in 1847.*

trends which were already developing, and one trend in the life of the court during Victoria's reign was the serious and high-minded approach to the world which at the end of the century was to feed liberal and Fabian ideas into the early labour movement. A surprising number of the most trusted members of the royal entourage were of this complexion. Sir Henry Ponsonby's son was to become leader of the Labour peers in the House of Lords, and the tutor to the Prince of Wales's children; Canon Dalton, who remained a lifelong friend of George v, was the father of Hugh Dalton, one of the outstanding leaders of the Labour Party, whose political career he appears to have approved and supported. The queen always involved herself in the appointment of the tutor to her two grandsons, the direct heirs to the throne after the Prince of Wales, and at one time this important post was apparently offered to Edward Carpenter. Carpenter of course was not then the well-known socialist that he later became, but he had been curate to F.D. Maurice, the prominent Christian socialist, and must therefore have had associations with precisely this kind of upper-middle-class liberal outlook which was one of the characteristic forms of radicalism in the second half of the century.

The queen always considered herself to be a liberal, and while it is difficult to see much in her later years that justified this view, it may perhaps be seen in this toleration of serious low church and radical ideas among her staff, as well as in the absence of 'aristocratic prejudices' of which Lord Esher spoke. Compared, for example, to her cousin and contemporary, the Duke of Cambridge, she was clearly in many ways more flexible and open to modern and liberal ideas. To some extent the court and the royal family were able to accept the greater seriousness as well as the close association with trade and business which were occurring among sections of the higher classes in society. They did not go to the extremes of religiosity and prudery with which they are sometimes credited. Their public demeanour was certainly more dignified and restrained than that of their immediate predecessors, and they never appeared publicly to endorse the more extravagant goings-on in the high life of the town or counties. Thus they may have been acceptable to a far wider section of the population than their contemporaries in more strictly stratified European societies. But the sources of the strength of the monarchy are complicated and must be sought not only in the personality and behaviour of the queen and her family, but in traditions and beliefs of the people and in the context in which alternative institutions were advocated.

The systems covered by the words 'republic' and 'monarchy' are not adequately described or identified by the terms. There may well be more in common in political terms between a republic and a monarchy than between any two republics or monarchies. Generalizations, therefore, about monarchy and republicanism in nineteenth-century

Europe have to be treated with care. The fact that so many of the industrialized democracies entered the twentieth century with a monarchical form of government shows that 'modernization' was as possible under a monarch as under a republic. If economic and political changes were not impeded by a constitutional monarchy, the presence of the institution could make national self-definition simpler and less contentious than racial, linguistic or religious forms of identity.

The nineteenth century saw changes in geographical boundaries, forms of government, methods of production, trade and finance, speed and means of transport and communication, with accompanying changes in consciousness and in the terms of political and other forms of discourse which many historians have grouped together under the term 'modernization'. Although the process started well before the nineteenth century, it was above all in this time that it reached its recognizable shape. 'Modernization' tends to be considered by those who use the term as more or less unqualified progress, and nation states of the twentieth century are judged by the degree to which they have become modernized. One of the great contradictions during the nineteenth century is the fact that Britain – in industrial developments certainly and in political and constitutional ones arguably the most rapidly modernizing state in Europe – remained, by its retention of an hereditary monarchy, in a state not merely of 'immaturity', but as one theoretician has expressed it, of 'infantility'. Setting aside for the moment the theological and emotional connotations of the concept of modernization, it remains of some interest not only that Britain, for all the rhetoric of developing parliamentary democracy and the growth of a meritocratic theory of advancement, retained an expensive hereditary monarchy, but that in none of the periods of political conflict during the century did a serious republican movement emerge – this in spite of the fact that in most of Europe and the rest of the world republicanism was a *sine qua non* of democratic politics.

Not that there were no republicans in nineteenth-century Britain. On the contrary, when pressed, a very large number – perhaps the majority – of radical, liberal and socialist political activists in all classes would probably have declared their attachment to a republican idea. In terms of practical politics, however, the abolition of the monarchy seldom appeared on the programme of party or faction. To some degree this is to be attributed to the particular circumstances of Victoria's accession and to her personality and perhaps most of all to her gender. But it has also to be considered as an aspect of the other main strand of nineteenth-century modernization, the growth of nationalism.

In many parts of Europe, nation states asserted their nationality and independence against the imperial control of an alien ruler. British nationalism asserted itself through attachment to an hereditary monarchy, rather than in opposition to an outside power. Wales and Scotland, nations with strong indigenous cultural and linguistic individuality, seem to have been won over, to varying degrees, to loyalty to the throne by the rather devious fictions of Welsh and Scottish ancestry among the royal antecedents. This loyalty was not evoked to the same extent in Ireland, where by the end of the century an active part of the Irish nationalist movement had reverted to the republicanism, if not to the political ideals of the United Irishmen. Even there, however, the most widely supported campaign of the century, the repeal movement led by Daniel O'Connell, swore allegiance to the queen and called only for a separate parliament under the crown.

As has already ben suggested, the lowest point in the popularity of the British monarchy in the century was probably in the years immediately preceding Victoria's accession. Most of the radicals and reformers of those days declared themselves to be republicans. They were followers and admirers of Thomas Paine and took their inspiration from the American and French revolutions. But another important radical influence in those years was the veteran reformer, Major Cartwright, whose formulation described the attitude of many of the early nineteenth-century radicals. In the words of his daughter,

> though in forming a new government in another part of the world, Major Cartwright would certainly have preferred a form of government as simply republican as would be consistent with security from anarchy, he never wished in his own country to interfere with its ancient constitutions.

The rhetoric of constitutionalism was used alongside the newer ideas of natural rights. In constitutional mythology, many of the past

heroes and heroines of the defence of British liberties were monarchs. In the summer of 1819, the month before the great reform
demonstration in St Peters Fields, Manchester, a radical poster
calling people to attend was headed 'BRITONS BE FREE' and
called on reformers to 'prove to the world that you are the country-
men of Boadicea, Alfred, Hampden, Sidney and Russell', including
male and female monarch, regicide and Commonwealthsmen in the
roll of honour.

Radicals did not hesitate to remind rulers, including the Prince
Regent, that heads had rolled and thrones changed occupancy when
monarchs had failed to 'shew a becoming deference for public
opinion and a little decent respect for the liberty of their subjects'.

The plebeian radical movement, even at its most confrontational,
was always anxious to retain the constitutional argument in its
armoury. By this argument the liberties of Englishmen were held to
be theirs by right and by tradition, with the function of the crown
being to protect and enlarge them. If kings or queens failed in that
duty, the people had a legal right – established in the seventeenth
century and reasserted since – to remove them and replace them with
more suitable figures. This argument may have rested on very shaky
foundations in history or in political theory, but it was a powerful
organizing concept. As has been shown, anti-royal feeling was much
more likely to take the form of an attack on a particular monarch than
an appeal to republicanism as such. There was rarely at any time
during the century a movement that united all republicans. The
ardent young Mazzinians of the first half of the century left little
trace, and turned away with disgust from the practical republicanism
of the later part of the century. As W.E. Adams wrote, remembering
the republicanism of his youth:

> It was not because a prince was temporarily unpopular, nor because
> the Monarchy was supposed to be expensive, that the young men of
> the fifties gave themselves to a republican propaganda. It was because,
> high above all sordid interests, there shone and flamed before them
> the ideal of an exalted and duteous people.

Adams's brand of republicanism produced one or two small journals
and a handful of radical writers, notably W.J. Linton and the
contributors to his *English Republic*, but it never sustained an

independent movement, remaining in effect a tendency among the more moderate supporters of the People's Charter.

After the first decade of Victoria's reign, republican and ultra-Hanoverian rhetoric alike declined. Although the queen's youth and her gender were seen by some of those in power as possibly weakening the institution of monarchy, they seem in fact to have been sources of strength from the beginning for those seeking to use the throne as a unifying force in the nation. There were contemporaries, at home and abroad, who saw the accession of a woman as a problem for the monarchy. Her two boy cousins, born in the same year as herself, had been christened George clearly with the throne in mind. 'George Cambridge', when told as a teenager that his cousin Victoria (whom he had described as 'a fat, ugly, wilful and stupid child') was heir to the throne, exclaimed 'Good heavens! A woman on the throne of so great a country – how ridiculous.' The Dean of Windsor, who may be presumed to have been a more disinterested, if no more tactful observer, congratulated the queen on the birth of the Prince of Wales in 1841, and thanked her for 'saving us from the incredible curse of a female succession'. For her less exalted subjects, however, as has been suggested, the young queen's gender may well have allayed republican sentiment at the time of her accession, and have affected republican politics for the rest of the century.

The nineteenth century was a period in which many of the middle class and the politically minded among the working class were concerned with the abolition of monopoly and privilege and with the achievement of a social ethic in which talent, merit and individual achievement were recognized and rewarded. A republican form of government might logically have been expected to figure on the programmes of any movements powered by these aims. Instead the monarchy was rarely questioned. Most of the movements for social reform saw the chief enemies of change among the landowning aristocracy, the great industrialists and financiers, or among the structures of privilege represented by the educational and military institutions which perpetuated the control of the ruling social groups. The extent to which the monarchy was involved with these institutions of power may well have been seriously underestimated by radical critics, but the result was that for most radicals republicanism was an issue of principle rather than of practical politics. Those who insisted on a republic as the only possible form of democracy remained for most of the century a purist, sectarian section of the movements of which they formed a part.

The claim of the Hanoverians to the throne rested on ideology as well as on legitimacy. The absolute right of the first in direct line of succession to reign had been overturned in 1688 and again in 1703 in the person of Queen Anne, who took precedence over her father and brother when she came to the throne. The constitutional manipulation of the succession had been managed in the past by the use of the female line, so that queens were sometimes associated not only with past 'golden ages' but with the victory of parliamentary government and Protestant ideology over legitimacy. An appeal to legitimacy was sometimes resorted to by those who felt particularly oppressed by the Hanoverian dominion, including of course Catholics and Scottish or Irish nationalists, but by the nineteenth century, there is almost no evidence of any serious popular Jacobitism. Perhaps the last manifestation was during the Irish rising of 1798, when the white Jacobite flag was glimpsed on a few occasions during the confused fighting. The articulate leadership of the rising was nationalist and strongly republican. For most of the nineteenth century, however, Irish nationalists tended to define their country as a 'kingdom', harking back to ancient traditions, or to be prepared to accept the British throne as the symbolic head of state if a separate Irish administration could be gained. Most English radicals in the nineteenth century do not seem to have looked back on the republic of the seventeenth century as any kind of golden age, while for the Irish the figure of Cromwell was almost the most hated in their whole demonology.

At the time of her accession, liberal and radical opinion saw support for Victoria as at least the lesser of two evils and a barrier against a more dangerous ruler. Overt republicanism assumed a low profile, therefore, and to some extent retained it during the Chartist period. The Chartists worded their demands in the language of constitutionalism, and were not above invoking the institution of the monarchy where it suited them. The call to the queen to dismiss her ministers was raised on more than one occasion, as were direct petitions to the throne. Rarely, however, does a tone of deference appear in Chartist speeches or writing, the constitutional issue is used in a purely instrumental manner, and the occasional press and platform references are almost uniformly critical, cynical or contemptuous, like that of the Merthyr Chartist, David Ellis, who remarked from the platform in 1843 that 'he had just heard that the Queen was in the family way again, and he supposed that that monkey was going to fill the Country with idlers'.

Chartism was a radical movement whose leaders and followers were in the main optimistic about the outcome of the campaign for the suffrage. The models of the successful campaign for Catholic Emancipation of 1828–9 and for the reform of Parliament in 1830–2 inspired the belief that a confident display of numbers in support of their claims, backed by open or implicit threats of disorder or violence if their demands were refused, could lead to the achievement of the People's Charter. The leadership, particularly the most popular and outstanding among the leaders, Feargus O'Connor, aimed at gaining the widest possible support and at avoiding issues which might divide radicals.

The accession of a young queen, recalling the Queen Caroline agitation and opposing in her person the claims of the Hanoverians, seemed to many radicals not only to be the lesser of two evils, but even to promise a new era of enlightened and uncorrupt politics. Sentimental popular royalism was invoked in the radical cause. One balladeer in the West Country, who was soon to be the publisher of local Chartist broadsides, issued a broadside ballad in 1837 which stressed the new monarch's liberal politics, but even more her gender. 'A New Song in Praise of Her Majesty Queen Victoria' contained eight stanzas and the refrain,

> Of all the flowers in full bloom,
> Adorn'd with beauty and perfume,
> The fairest is the rose of June,
> Victoria Queen of England.

It began:

> Welcome now Victoria,
> Welcome to the Royal throne,
> May all trades soon begin to stir,

> Beloved Queen of England.
> For your most gracious Majesty,
> May see what dreadful poverty,
> Is to be found in England's ground
> Beloved Queen of England,

and went on to outline a programme for the new monarch and to put into her mouth expressions which might have amazed her.

> When o'er the country you preside,
> Providence will be your guide,
> The people then will never chide
>   Victoria Queen of England.
> She doth declare it's her intent,
> To extend Reform of Parliament.
> On doing good she's fully bent
>   While she is Queen of England
>   Of all the flowers etc.
>
> She says I'll try my utmost skill,
> That the poor may have their fill,
> Forsake them, no, I never will,
>   While I am Queen of England;
> For oft my mother said to me,
> Let this your study always be,
> To see your people blest and free,
>   Should you be Queen of England.
>
> I will encourage every trade,
> For his labour each must be paid,
> In this free country then said –
>   Victoria Queen of England.
> That poor law Bill with many more
> Will soon be trampled on the floor,
> The rich must keep the helpless poor
>   Now Victoria's Queen of England.

The final stanza declared:

> In every town and village gay,
> Upon her Coronation day,
> The bells shall ring and music play,
>   For Victoria Queen of England.
> While her affections we do win,
> And every day fresh tidings bring,
> Ladies help me for to sing,
>   Victoria Queen of England.

Peter Murray McDouall, a Chartist leader who was among the most consistent advocates of physical force doctrines, and who edited his own *Chartist and Republican Journal*, also wrote a 'Poetical Petition to Queen Victoria on Behalf of the Oppressed Working Classes of Great Britain and in Demand of their Political Rights and Liberty', in which he reminded her that

> That jewelled crown upon thy youthful head
> Was chased and wrought by men who pine for bread,

and appealed to her better nature to intervene on behalf of her poorer subjects. McDouall's abject behaviour was noted with sorrow by the republican W.J. Linton, yet if we are to suggest a left–right spectrum of beliefs and policies among leading Chartists, there can be no doubt that McDouall was some way to the left of Linton. He openly advocated a resort to arms, and indeed sacrificed career, money and health throughout his life to his devotion to radical working-class politics.

There is no great mystery in these years about the devotion of the wealthier classes in Britain to the monarchy. From the seventeenth century onwards the personal power of the monarch had been trimmed to prevent royal interference with the processes of government so that, as Professor Cannon has pointed out, by the nineteenth century the British regime was one which the seventeenth-century Stuarts, or indeed most eighteenth- and nineteenth-century European monarchs, would hardly recognize as a monarchy at all. In so far as there was dissatisfaction with Victoria among the higher orders it was either anti-female or pro-Hanoverian. Not until the second half of the century did an active bourgeois republican trend develop; the historical puzzle is the low priority given to republicanism among radicals, especially in the turbulent years of the first half of the century.

Opposition or hostility to the throne took one of three main forms during Victoria's reign. The first, what might be called 'pure' republicanism, was always to be found, but seldom on any platform. The second, the support for an alternative candidate for the throne, existed as a position of the extreme right at the time of Victoria's accession and was to emerge in other forms later in her reign. This does not seem to have been a major ingredient of popular politics, except in so far as it was a male-chauvinist attitude. It is an interesting element in the rhetoric of popular politics, however, that in a century in which male dominion and the separation of spheres into sharply defined male and female areas became entrenched in the ideology of all classes, a female in the highest office in the nation seems to have been almost universally accepted.

The third kind of anti-royal rhetoric, and by far the most widespread and influential, was the *ad personam* attack on the cost of royalty, often directed against particular royal expenditure or against the cost of the royal family or the royal household. This kind of irreverent criticism was not exactly republicanism, although it was used extensively by republicans, but in its demystification of royalty and its insistence on the accountability of the crown in mundane matters of money and behaviour it probably represented the greatest threat to the monarchy. An atmosphere of disgust and condemnation of a particular monarch at a time when no acceptable alternative was in sight was the most likely situation in which a British republic might have emerged in the nineteenth century. It is for this reason that Victoria's existence and her personality were so important in 1837. It was also to affect her attitude to her eldest son, the heir to the throne, and to be in the background in the early 1870s, the only other period in the century in which the republican alternative seemed a possible one.

The class polarization of the 1840s and the lowering of the profile of the Hanoverian threat meant that the Chartists began to employ anti-royal rhetoric more and more. The arrival of another child was announced as 'The birth of another royal tax-eater' in the *Northern Star* and the award of a grant towards national education which was less than that given in the same year to the royal stables was constantly cited. The second Chartist petition, presented to the House of Commons in 1842 specifically criticized 'the salaries of those whose comparative usefulness ought to be questioned' and went on to comment,

> That your petitioners, with all due respect and loyalty, would compare the daily income of the Sovereign Majesty with that of thousands of working men of this nation; and whilst your petitioners have learned

THE ROYAL BILL OF EXPENCES.

Vic.—Dear Father Bull—ahem—I have sent for you merely to show you that—that—that—ahem—that—(aside) "Oh, Ah, how shall I bring it out?"—I'm—I'm—I'm very much in DEBT, and here is the account of my expenses during these last two years (unfolding it).

BULL. (Startled, and with hair on end.) The L—d have mercy on me!!! well, I never! And so, ma'am, after my pockets are yearly drained, to pay you HALF-A-MILLION for the support and pleasure of you and your household, there is impudence enough left in you to saddle me with that endless bill of your new debts? Well, if this don't beat all! (looking at it.) What's that? Opera Expences ; but I don't see English Drama Expences. And then the journey to Scotland— to France—to Belgium—to the Midland Counties—and—what's that? Masked Balls—Foreign Artistes! There's no debts incurred though through visiting the Poor of our own Land. It seems all for pleasures—I'm tired of looking at it!!

PEEL. (Through the door.) The old fool is always grumbling.

Apart from small republican journals, most of the critics of the throne concentrated on the cost to the taxpayer and on the foreignness of the Prince Consort.

that her Majesty receives daily for her private use the sum of £164 17s 10d., they have also ascertained that many thousands of the families of the labourers are only in receipt of 3¾d. per head per day;

They commented in addition on Prince Albert's daily £104 2s. and recorded their 'astonishment' at the £57 10s. daily allocated to the King of Hanover.

But the existence of a woman on the throne was also used to call for the admission of women to the political system, as Disraeli noticed when he put the argument into the mouth of Caroline, the Chartist factory girl in *Sybil*:

> 'It's fine news for a summer day . . . to say we can't understand politics with a Queen on the throne.'
> 'She's got her ministers to tell her what to do,' said Mrs Carey, taking a pinch of snuff. 'Poor innocent young creature, it often makes my heart ache to think how she is beset.'
> 'Over the left,' said Julia. 'If the ministers try to come into her bedchamber, she knows how to turn them to the right about.'

Three decades after the publication of the novel, Disraeli was again to invoke the crown as a popular symbol, although this time in support of the status quo, and not as a model for women's political emancipation. When he was writing *Sybil* in 1844, however, he was picking up the argument from a wide reading of the political arguments of the Chartists.

The politics of Chartism were empirical and specific. The demand for the admission of men of no property to the political system assumed that a considerable range of social and political change would follow such admission. To some, like Linton and Adams, the republic would follow the Charter, for monarchy would be unable to survive in the age of democracy. The Charter, however, took priority over all other measures. When the Second Republic was established in February 1848 in France, it was greeted with enormous enthusiasm by the Chartists, but with the slogan, 'France has the Republic, England must have the Charter'.

Although it is not difficult to find republican sentiments being articulated by Chartist speakers and writers, it is probable that most Chartists held the view of the monarchy contained in Ernest Jones's poem 'The Revolt of Hindostan', written in prison in 1849–50, and dedicated to 'The People of the United Queendom and of the United States', the latter addressed as 'free citizens of the republic', the former as 'unenfranchised subjects of the monarchy'. The poem is a utopian vision of the future, after a revolution against the European empires by their subjects, led by India. In defeated Britain,

> While prostrate mercy raised her drooping head,
> Thus came the People, thus the gold-kings fled;
> None fought for them – none spoke: they slunk away,
> Like guilty shadows at appearing day;
> They were not persecuted – but forgot:
> Their place was vacant, and men missed them not.
> And Royalty, that dull and outworn tool!
> Bedizened doll upon a gilded stool –
> The seal that Party used to stamp an Act
> Vanished in form, as it had long in fact.

The monarchy, for Jones, was a residual feature of an older form of society which would die a natural death once a democratic parliamentary system was established.

Jones's assessment was shared by most of his fellow radicals. They almost certainly underestimated the personal power of Victoria and of Albert, but even so their assessment was not a totally naive one. In his dedication of the poem, Jones warns the Americans of the dangers of centralizing governmental power and of the great increase that was taking place in the power of capital in their republic, and it was these questions in Britain which always concerned the Chartists more than the power of the crown.

The Chartists, then, although in many cases believing in a republican ideal, never directed their main propaganda against the throne. They felt threatened by an exclusive political system, a centralizing state and the increasing control exercised over their work and their lives by merchant and manufacturing capital. The throne, occupied by a young female, was, to begin with at least, as likely to be invoked on the side of traditional liberties, in the name of Alfred or Boadicea, as to be represented as an oppressive or parasitical institution. When Chartist speakers did attack the queen, it was more likely to be in the language of carnival or satire than of serious politics. 'Little Vic' came in for plenty of snide comments about her fecundity and her wealth, whilst even the most internationally-minded among the Chartist speakers was not above the occasional anti-German crack at the time of her marriage. The

A CASE OF REAL DISTRESS.

"Good People, pray take compassion upon us. It is now nearly seven years since we have either of us known the blessing of a Comfortable Residence. If you do not believe us, good people, come and see where we live, at Buckingham Palace, and you will be satisfied that there is no deception in our story. Such is our Distress, that we should be truly grateful for the blessing of a comfortable two-pair back, with commonly decent sleeping Rooms for our Children and Domestics. With our slender means, and an increasing Family, we declare to you that we do not know what to do. The sum of One Hundred and Fifty Thousand Pounds will be all that will be required to make the needful alterations in our dwelling. Do, good people, bestow your Charity to this little amount, and may you never live to feel the want of so small a triple."

The royal family begging for a mere £150,000 for a new house
(Punch, *1846*).

serious republicans like Linton and Adams disliked both the appeal to tradition and the *ad personam* arguments. All these attitudes to the monarchy were to surface again in radical and republican movements later in the century.

The Jacobin, Chartist and Republican ideals of the early nineteenth century tended to go with a deep distrust of all centralizing politics, including some kinds of socialism. For the writers of the *English Republic*, the true republic could only be founded on ideals of liberty, equality and fraternity. As Linton wrote,

Socialism is not always republican. The socialism which would make the State (and let it be the government of even a majority, and however great that majority) the director and dictator of labour with only this change from our present system – that the workman would be under, instead of the tyranny of single or combined capitalists, the stronger tyranny of a corporate majority; . . . such socialism would not be republican.

The throne, for radicals in the first sixty years of the nineteenth century, was a vulgar but marginal institution which would disappear almost without effort once the deeper and more fundamental problems of society had been solved.

6

THE REPUBLICAN
ALTERNATIVE
2   1861–1901

IN 1792 Tom Paine had predicted seven years' future life for the British monarchy. In 1871 Joseph Chamberlain wrote to Charles Dilke, 'The Republic must come, and at the rate at which we are moving, it will come in our generation.' Radical politicians were again beginning to see the institution of monarchy as irrational and unnecessary. Chamberlain and some of his associates near the centres of government had particular reasons to consider both the queen and her heir apparent to be candidates for a quiet and diplomatic withdrawal from public life. For working-class radicals French experience led the way, as it had done in the 1790s. *Fraser's Magazine* in the spring of 1871 reported that in London,

> Men – decent steady artisans . . . speaking amid applauding circles of shopmates wished that the whole tribe of Royalty were under the sod; while women, mothers themselves, prayed that its women might be made unfruitful, so that the race of royal paupers might not be increased.

Twenty years after the end of Chartism, working-class radicals began to look again at republican politics. At the same time the British republic appeared on the agenda of active bourgeois politicians.

The change in atmosphere was closely connected with the behaviour of the monarch. Radicals in the fifties and sixties had not been very much concerned with the throne. Ernest Jones, the last of the major Chartist leaders, who had emerged in the sixties as a leader of the movement for the further reform of Parliament, had taken part in 1867 in a famous debate with Professor Blackie of Edinburgh on democracy. He defended universal suffrage and democratic institutions against the professor's elitist arguments, but in the course of the debate claimed that 'there may be democracy under a king as well as under a president'. He objected to Blackie's use of French experience to attack democracy in Britain, refusing a comparison between the two countries,

> France, where licentious tyranny mocked at every virtue and trampled on every right, and Britain where the virtues of the throne are but an emblem of the virtues of the nation; between the land of Charles the Ninth and Louis Quinze, and the empire of Elizabeth and Queen Victoria.

For Jones's father, Victoria had been the only hope for Britain of avoiding a corrupt tyranny. For Jones himself she stood for the public virtues by which democracy was encouraged and sustained. Ernest Jones died in 1869, before the Paris Commune and the revival of republicanism in Britain. He does, however, express some of the disillusion felt by British radicals at the outcome of the 1848 revolution in France and the failure there of the panacea of universal manhood suffrage. An hereditary monarch, particularly a woman, may well have seemed less of a threat to the development of a democratic state than an elected president whose political power was, by virtue of his very election, so much greater.

The late sixties and early seventies, however, saw an awakening both of republicanism and of anti-royalism. The death of Albert, the rise of John Brown and the queen's avoidance of the public duties of her office coincided with events in Europe which again brought republicanism into the political arena. There was a lobby which considered that the queen had ruled for long enough and that now her proper behaviour, as a widow, was to step down and allow the male heir to assume the throne. There was also, particularly among metropolitan politicians who had some knowledge of the prince and his behaviour, a strong and growing movement for straightforward republicanism. It was at first led by Sir Charles Dilke and was supported by a group of MPs and by many non-parliamentary liberals including the positivists Frederick Harrison and Edward Beesly. The latent republicanism of working-class radicalism was undoubtedly awakened by the Paris Commune, and for a short time the throne in Britain appeared again under threat, through a combination of external events and the personal behaviour of the monarch.

GEORGE

PRINCE OF WALES,

WITH RECENT CONTRASTS AND COINCIDENCES.

BY

CHARLES BRADLAUGH.

———

LONDON:
PUBLISHED AT 17, JOHNSON'S COURT, FLEET ST., E.C.
———
PRICE TWOPENCE.

One of the few republican pamphlets that are still remembered is Charles Bradlaugh's Impeachment of the House of Brunswick *(1872). It began with this much shorter account of George* IV's *period as Prince of Wales, which was a thinly disguised attack on the current holder of the title.*

In 1870, the republican journalist and politician Charles Bradlaugh drew an obvious moral from the fact that the queen had fulfilled few of her public duties since the death of the Prince Consort. 'The experience of the last nine years,' he wrote, 'proves that the country can do quite well without a monarch and may therefore save the extra expense of monarchy.' The issue of the cost of the royal family became a constant theme among critics of the throne, even some who would not have advocated the complete abolition of the institution. A recent essay on attitudes to Queen Victoria in Wales has shown this to have been almost the only form of anti-royal expression found in Wales until nearly the end of the reign. It was certainly the almost invariable lead-in to 'respectable' middle-class republicanism. Two of the most widely distributed pamphlets of the 1870s, the anonymously published *What does she do with it?* often attributed to George Otto Trevelyan and Charles Bradlaugh's *Impeachment of the House of Brunswick*, based their argument largely on the cost of the royals to the taxpayer. Such an argument had particular force at a time when the queen's visibility was low, her family expenses great and increasing, and the character of her apparent successor extremely suspect. Chamberlain's assessment might well have seemed a reasonable one, not necessarily involving revolutionary or even ultra-radical politics. In a famous address on the subject in Newcastle in 1871, Sir Charles Dilke expressed the view that the end of the monarchy was to be expected:

> If you can show me a fair chance that a republic here will be free from the political corruption that hangs about the monarchy, I say, for my part – and I believe the middle classes in general will say – let it come.

The republicanism of Liberal politicians was welcomed publicly by some of the few remaining Chartist republicans like George Julian Harney and the radical newspaper owner, Joseph Cowen of Newcastle, but the form it took did not appeal to the committed idealists among them. Remembering the period at the end of the century, W.E. Adams, by then editor of Cowen's *Newcastle Weekly Chronicle*, condemned both the message and the messenger: 'What . . . was the worth of that paltry cry about the Cost of the Crown, raised by Sir Charles Dilke before his own tremendous lapse?'

There was, however, more to the republicanism of that moment than the Chamberlain/Dilke approach. Looking back from 1901, James Ramsey MacDonald recalled those years as a time when

> the throne seemed to be tottering . . . the Queen and the Prince of Wales had no hold on the popular mind; there was a spirit of democratic independence abroad; the common man believed in the common man.

The Annuity of £15,000 of the public moneys
to Prince Arthur.

THE COST

OF THE

Royal Household,

ROYAL ANNUITIES,

AND

CROWN LANDS.

By J. CHARLES COX.

(TWELFTH THOUSAND.)

PRICE ONE PENNY.

DERBY:

W. & W. PIKE & SON, *REPORTER* OFFICE.

LONDON: E. TRUELOVE, 256, High Holborn. MANCHESTER: J. HEYWOOD.
SHEFFIELD: A. SULLIVAN, Snig Hill. NOTTINGHAM: J. SWEET,
Stoney Street.

The years 1869 to 1872 saw a flood of republican pamphlets, nearly all of them linked to financial questions relating to the increasing cost of Victoria's family.

Keir Hardie, future leader of the Independent Labour Party, grew up in a household dominated by the 'Bradlaughism' of his mother and stepfather. Bradlaugh's atheism as well as his republicanism were in some ways an embarrassment to Hardie as a child, but he recalled that his first political memory was of the active republican clubs in the north of England and Scotland in 1871, and he took with him into his political career the republicanism, if not the atheism, of his parents' home.

In the organizations and in the publications of the radical and working-class left in the late sixties and early seventies, republicanism was on the increase. A journal named *The Republican* appeared in 1870, following two others of the same name that had appeared earlier in the century, one edited by Richard Carlile in the 1820s and the other by C.G. Harding in 1848. The name had been out of use since the mid-century, but a writer in the labour and reforming journal *The Commonwealth* caught the new spirit and reminded its readers that 'Commonwealth' was in English synonymous with 'republic'. The combination of disillusion with the limited results of the 1867 Reform Act, severe social distress – in which pauperism and unemployment reached levels unknown in Britain since 1848 – and above all the overthrow of the French Second Empire lent a republican tone to almost all the agitation and activity of the years between 1869 and 1872.

An examination of the republican propaganda of these years, however, reveals a familiar pattern. It was indeed now possible to speak openly about a British republic, but few of the politicians in any class who did so put its achievement at the top of their agenda. For Bradlaugh the monarchy was part of the obscurantism and mystification which bedevilled British life, but his targets included the church and the medical establishment. He was, however, among the most firmly committed to republicanism: a New York paper saw him as 'the coming Cromwell' and credited his London Republican Club with 30,000 members. The members of the Land and Labour League appeared at a demonstration on behalf of the unemployed on Good Friday 1870 wearing

> broad scarlet sashes, not over the shoulder, but around the waist, in the exact pattern current among the *sans culottes* of the first French Revolution, and, in a further imitation of that class, poles were borne aloft with the emblematical caps of liberty.

But although they were a staunchly republican body, their concern was more with their programme of land nationalization and other major social and economic reforms than with republicanism.

The movement, if it could ever have been called one, disintegrated rapidly into groups whose only common interest – the desire to be rid of the monarchy – was insufficient to mount a joint campaign.

Perhaps the 'retired widow and unemployed youth' of Bagehot's famous 1867 phrase did not represent a sufficiently positive obstacle to social or political reform to inspire a strong demonstration of public hostility.

These years also represented one of the very lowest points in the century for working-class activity of any kind, so that there was no wider movement to pick up and incorporate the feelings of alienation from and dissatisfaction with the queen and her offspring. By the time a genuine labour movement had developed in the last two decades of the century, the image and the public standing of the monarchy had recovered to a degree that few would have foreseen in 1871.

Nevertheless, the republicanism of the late sixties and early seventies sent signals to her advisers that loyalty to the queen was under strain from a number of directions. At one end of the spectrum was sheer boredom. The queen had been in retirement since the death of her husband, she was not fulfilling even the minimal public functions of her office and there were clearly many who felt that the nation required someone more colourful and energetic as a symbol. This argument was used often by Dilke and his supporters, who argued from the queen's inactivity that she could well be dispensed with. Even outside republican circles, the proposal that the queen should make way for her son and accept the dignified role of a dowager was regularly mooted.

This merged into the view of many practical liberal politicians that now was the time quietly to rid the country altogether of the encumbrance of a useless monarchy. Apart from the queen's own lack of lustre the increasing demands made on the public funds by the royal family created considerable hostility. In 1858 the Princess Victoria had married the heir to the throne of Prussia. In the same year her youngest sister, Beatrice, was born. Queen Victoria demanded a dowry of £80,000 and an annuity of £10,000 for her eldest daughter, which Parliament reduced to £40,000 and £8,000. Even those figures, however, seemed to many to be enormous sums to be paid for an alliance with a country which already seemed increasingly hostile. The prospect of similar demands for all the remaining royal children, eight of them at the time of Vicky's

AN HISTORICAL PARALLEL;
ELIZABETH—1589.

OR, COURT PASTIMES.
VICTORIA—1845.

Prince Albert here appears as both foreign and barbaric. His passion for deer-shooting certainly did result in a vast slaughter of game, as did the regular royal shoots.

marriage, with no guarantee then that the series was at an end, did nothing to endear the monarchy to the tax-paying public.

Throughout the sixties this grievance persisted, and the Franco-Prussian war of 1870 highlighted the unpopularity of assumed royal support for Prussia. A lacklustre and very expensive royal family, allied to and therefore implicitly involving the British nation with unpopular foreign royal figures, made the possibility of a republican alternative through the inanition of the monarchy a real one. Add to this the enthusiasm among labour and radical leaders for the positive declaration of a republic in response to the overthrow of the French emperor and to the events of the Paris Commune, and for the first time since her accession, Victoria's throne seemed under serious threat.

The fact that the unpopularity of the monarchy did not occur at a
time of very great activity in radical politics as a whole underlines the
extent to which the institution of the monarchy was separated in the
public mind from domestic politics. Had the queen's or the prince's
behaviour been associated with political rather than with moral or
familial failings, or had there been in the country generally a strong
movement of hostility to the established political rulers that might
have gained strength from the unpopularity of the monarchy, this
could have been the time when a British republic emerged. There is
no doubt that it was a low point for the crown's popularity. His
involvement in a much publicized divorce case, the Mordaunt affair,
made the Prince of Wales a less than usually enticing candidate for
the throne. The queen's association with John Brown was the subject
of indignation or innuendo, according to choice, so that the 'retired
widow and unemployed youth' began to be seen as being less
innocuously occupied than the phrase might seem to imply. Gladstone noted in a memorandum to the Foreign Secretary that the fund
of goodwill towards the queen and her son was diminishing,

> and I do not see from whence it is to be replenished as matters go now.
> To speak in rude and general terms, the Queen is invisible and the
> Prince of Wales is not respected.

With attitudes towards the crown varying from boredom through distrust to outright hostility, the ground was ready for a revival of republicanism. The 1867 Reform Bill and the agitation which preceded it
occupied liberal and labour politicians for most of the sixties, but
although a new social group – the artisans and well-established working people in the towns – were admitted to the parliamentary system,
the results brought little joy to the majority of the working population.
The last years of the decade saw great hardship and unemployment,
and also the revival of directly republican propaganda and activity.

But republicanism was supported for the most part by groups and
individuals who lacked political power and influence. Although the
Liberals were beginning in the seventies to seek support from the
newly-enfranchised urban artisans on some aspects of trade union
and labour policy, they were not interested in listening to them on
wider questions of domestic or foreign policy. The small group of
parliamentary republicans were not for the most part men who could

easily lead a moral campaign against the extravagance of the throne, since some, like Dilke and Labouchere, themselves belonged to versions of the 'fast' set patronized by the Prince of Wales, and all, since members of Parliament were still unpaid, were men of considerable independent means. The latent republicanism among the lower classes needed to be allied with political programmes more concerned with their own needs to bring them out on the streets or – after 1872 – to the ballot box.

The most important and influential of the politicians who espoused the cause of republicanism in these years was undoubtedly Joseph Chamberlain. His biographer maintained that Chamberlain's republicanism did not amount to much, although it clearly stirred up some controversy among Liberal politicians at the time. A brief look at his experience as a republican advocate illustrates some of the traps which the subject held for politicians.

At the time of the fall of the French Second Empire in 1870 Chamberlain, then in his middle thirties, addressed a meeting in the town hall of his home city of Birmingham. He declared:

> For my part, I do not feel any great horror at the idea . . . of the possible establishment of a Republic in this country. [Loud cheers] I am quite certain that sooner or later it will come. [Renewed cheers and 'Bravo'] But there is really not any great practical difference between a free constitutional monarchy such as ours and a free republic.

In later speeches, he referred to the coming of a republic 'some day', and for a short time he was clearly involved with his friend Dilke in something approaching the active promotion of republicanism. In 1872, when he agreed to attend – indeed to preside over – a meeting to promote the further reform of Parliament which had been organized by a committee of radical societies and trade unions, he attended as a delegate of a number of local reform associations, including the Birmingham Republican Club. Dilke says in his memoirs that Chamberlain 'joined republican clubs', although Chamberlain's biographer denies this.

But whether or not he was actually a member of the clubs which he represented, his representation brought down attacks on him as a red republican from friends and political associates. In response to these attacks he refrained from supporting Dilke on the matter of the civil

list, and went out of his way at a Liberal dinner, to propose 'the
Health of the Queen'. In his speech on that occasion he reiterated his
belief that republicanism was the best principle 'for a free and
enlightened people', but went on to say,

> I am not prepared to enter into an agitation in order to upset the
> existing state of things, to destroy the Monarchy and to change the
> name of the titular ruler of this country.

The diners then sang 'God Save the Queen'.

It is usually said that the main reason for the rapid death of the
republican agitation in these years was the illness of the Prince of
Wales in the winter of 1871. It may be that the republicans were, at
their strongest, a rational and vocal minority, but that the affair of the
prince's illness brought to the surface feelings of loyalty among the
usually unvocal and inarticulate. Certainly the atmosphere created by
Bertie's illness and recovery was one in which talk of abolishing the
monarchy became extremely difficult. He fell ill in December 1871 of
typhoid fever, the disease which was generally believed to have killed
his father exactly ten years earlier. The news was soon spread by the
press, and the nation heard of his serious condition, and of the queen's
vigil by his Sandringham sick-bed. Aided, as his father had not been,
by a rapid and correct diagnosis and by skilful nursing, the prince
passed through the crisis of his illness and made a rapid and complete
recovery. Crowds on the street and loyal messages of all kinds greeted
the news. An indication of the changed atmosphere can be seen in the
fact that a vote in Parliament to reduce the annuity of one of his royal
brothers, Prince Arthur, had received 53 votes a few months before
his illness, while in March the next year Dilke could only find two
supporting votes for an inquiry into the civil list.

The Liberal republicans thus found themselves isolated in Parliament and under attack from many of their supporters. Working-class
radicals seemed more prepared to follow Gladstone on central issues
like free trade and the reform of trade union law than to support the
maverick republicans in the Liberal Party.

It is interesting to speculate on the assertion made by Kingsley
Martin in his study of the monarchy that had Gladstone embraced
the republican cause he could have 'lighted a republican bonfire that
would have consumed Buckingham Palace, Windsor Castle and

Balmoral too'. Gladstone was a strong monarchist and never, in Lady Ponsonby's words, 'showed his teeth' about his treatment by the queen or his doubts about the royal house. It cannot, however, be assumed that had he thought otherwise he could have taken his wide popular following with him, even at the height of his popularity as 'the People's William'. Among his more radical colleagues there was considerable hesitation about the expression of outright republican views. John Bright, Reform League and Anti-Corn-Law League leader, when told in 1872 that some English republicans wished him to be the first president, responded cautiously, echoing, no doubt unconsciously, the argument of Major Cartwright:

> As to *opinions* on the question of Monarchy or Republicanism, I hope and believe it will be a long time before we are asked to give our opinion; our ancestors decided the matter a long time since, and I would suggest that you and I should leave any further decision to our posterity.

Although not a convinced royalist like Gladstone, Bright not only declined to tackle the hot potato of republicanism, but on one occasion at least spoke out publicly in defence of the queen when fellow-radicals criticized her withdrawal from public life. He defended her as a woman:

> A woman – be she the Queen of a great realm, or be she the wife of one of your labouring men – who can keep alive in her heart a great sorrow for the lost object of her life and affection is not at all likely to be wanting in a great and generous sympathy for you.

Had Victoria stepped down when her son came of age in the early sixties, the history of the monarchy might have been different. Her own realization of this possibility made her decide to continue during her widowhood and old age in the public role of head of state. It was a decision which went against the dominating view of women's social and domestic role, a view with which she herself clearly had much sympathy. Criticisms of her decision were themselves muted by the respect which the same dominating ideology demanded for her gender. Her gender also provided the basis for her re-emergence as a national symbol in the late seventies and eighties.

After 1871 republicanism rapidly lost its attraction as part of the platform of Liberal politicians. The fury of the response to public criticisms of the royal family was not worth provoking for the small political advantage that a principled stand might offer. Even those most critical of the conduct of the queen and the Prince of Wales, hesitated to make public *ad personam* attacks which could not be answered by the victims. It was above all ungentlemanly and in very bad taste to make public criticisms of a female. It is clear that many among the upper classes spoke in an extremely ungentlemanly way about the queen in private. William Morris, for example, well before his conversion to socialism, when he was part of a group of intellectuals and others working to avoid British involvement in a war in the near East, always referred to the queen in his private letters as 'Mrs Brown'. While Albert was alive the royal couple were referred to as 'Joseph and Eliza' by superior upper-class subjects who found their middle-class style trying, and the widespread use of 'Mrs Brown' or the later 'Empress Brown' was even less respectful.

As far as public organization went, republican clubs survived into the 1870s in London, Birmingham, Nottingham, Sheffield, Northampton, Newcastle, Jarrow and Middlesbrough. They seem mainly to have been supported by the same clientele as the free-thinking and atheist organizations. With Bradlaugh as their leader, this is hardly surprising, but the overlap also suggests a similarity of approach between the two movements. Their supporters were men and women of a logical turn of mind, firmly opposed to superstition of all kinds, and equally to mass campaigning on emotive or sentimental issues. As the secularist and ex-Chartist H.V. Mayer put it, demonstrations were only to be held on major occasions, and

> they must be conducted logically and decorously, and the less it has to do with red caps and red flags the better; I know how Chartism suffered from a similar policy and I have no desire to see Republicanism share a similar fate.

It is hardly surprising, therefore, that their sedate campaign was by the mid-seventies making very few waves. At the time of the wedding of Prince Leopold, Victoria's youngest son, in 1882, the *Secular Review* fell back on the old line of personal attack, and W.S. Ross inveighed against

> the German king-factory, which factory seems to have a monopoly of turning out microcephalous mediocrities with an inimitable blend of

insatiable cupidity. Each of these Hanoverian trinkets, including the elderly invisible one have a crack on the top of their heads suited for the dropping in of half-crowns, and millions of half-crowns are dropped into their cranial crack even by starving wretches who cannot get bread.

The compositors of the journal on this occasion refused to set the article so the typesetting had to be done by the author and the editor.

In the middle of the seventies interest in the monarchy was revived and the public presence of the queen and her son made more colourful and lively by the active policies of politicians, particularly by Disraeli. But even before this the short-lived flare of republicanism seems to have burnt itself out. The Great British Public refused to see the throne as threatening anything but its pocket, and seems to have found even this threat worth no more than the odd grumble when extra money was required for royal family endowments. Disraeli's move in creating the title of Empress of India for the queen in 1876, and the celebrations of her golden jubilee in 1887 and diamond jubilee a decade later, meant that there was a grand royal event in each of the last three decades of the century – events which highlight the growing imperial power of Britain. A series of royal occasions – weddings, births and christenings among her children and grandchildren – kept the royal pageant reasonably well to the fore in these decades of peace between the great powers and of commercial and industrial expansion.

The labour movement which began to take shape in the last two decades of the nineteenth century was the first republican movement in Britain in modern times. Unlike the *ad hoc* republicanism of the seventies, the labour movement grew out of two strong political traditions; one was the 'Jacobin' tradition of the rights of man, political and citizenship rights and opposition to privilege and monopoly, the other the philosophy of socialism based on a belief in social equality and the community control of resources. Neither of these traditions could logically accommodate an hereditary monarchy with great private wealth supported by national taxation. The early labour and socialist leaders took the abolition of the monarchy as one of the inevitable results of a socialist transformation, whether peaceful or violent. As the biographer of one of the greatest of them put it,

> He [Keir Hardie] was certainly a Republican, but like most Socialists he regarded the Monarchy as simply an appanage of the political and social system, which would disappear as a matter of course when the system disappeared.

Hardie came into national political life at around the time of the queen's golden jubilee. This was the occasion of a brief republican revival. The year, 1887, was a depressed one for trade and employment, and there was inevitably the sense that the jubilee was an essay in bread and circuses without the bread. At Llanelly, 'Her Majesty's name was received with groans and hisses' at a public meeting, while the Cardiff Trades Council refused 'to do anything in the shape of servile admiration of a well-paid servant of the State'. When the unemployed workmen took a leaf out of the Chartists' book and organized marches to their parish churches, demanding sermons from the incumbent on texts with radical implications, they were often met by clergy determined to turn the occasion in the other direction. In the golden-jubilee year the unemployed of Deptford in South London were treated to a sermon on the text 'Let every soul be subject to the higher powers', and could record their protest only by hissing the names of the queen and the Prince of Wales during the prayers.

Republicans and radicals took advantage of the jubilee to reiterate the case against the monarchy, but again, the mixture of *ad personam* abuse of the queen and her son with serious questions of principle was an uneasy one. Hardie, on an early visit to London, attended a meeting of the Social Democratic Federation on the evening of the queen's jubilee. One speaker, Hardie wrote, called the queen

> 'that old woman who had never so much as spent ten minutes washing a shirt for her husband in return for all the money she has received.' His audience cheered him to the echo and, after the meeting was over, robbed themselves of their manhood by swilling in a public house. I took the opportunity of stating a few wholesome truths and reminded the meeting that, before we could have Socialism we must have a fit and prepared people. Had I to choose between the autocratic rule of the Emperor of Russia and the democratic rule of an unprincipled, ignorant mob, I would, by preference, choose the former as the better of the two – and I speak as an extreme Democrat.

It may be noted that the occupation which the SDF members felt to be appropriate for an old woman might not have appealed to women socialists, who were clearly not of the company that night.

The Socialist League, William Morris's group, maintained a high-minded and principled attitude to the monarchy. An editorial in their journal, *Commonweal*, declared, 'We assume as a matter of course that a government of privileged persons, hereditary and commercial, cannot act usefully or rightly towards the community; their position forbids it.' Nevertheless,

> as to mere politics, Absolutism, Constitutionalism, Republicanism have all been tried in our day and under our present social system, and have all alike failed in dealing with the real evils of life.

For all this, however, the sheer ostentation and vulgarity of the jubilee inspired Morris to polemic. At the end of the week's celebration he reminded his readers that a middle-class dominated republic would be no better for the working people, but went on to say,

> Nevertheless, now the monstrous stupidity is on us . . . one's indignation swells pretty much to the bursting-point . . . We must not after all forget what the hideous, revolting and vulgar tomfoolery in question really means nowadays.

In her old age the queen was fairly impervious to personal attacks, and was perceived increasingly as some kind of mother-figure throughout Britain and the Empire. The Prince of Wales was another matter. The queen's constant doubts about his suitability for the role he was to assume seemed to be borne out by his behaviour. He led a life of self-indulgent pleasure-seeking in London, Paris and at various country houses. He was involved in scandals and near-scandals associated with cards or with women; the fashionable world rang with mildly scandalous stories about him. The queen feared for the succession and was not alone in her fears. 'How long will it last, we wonder?' asked the *Pall Mall Gazette* in the week of the 1887 jubilee. 'As long as the Queen lasts, yes, but after the Queen, who knows?'

7

JUBILEE YEARS

THE fact that the monarch was a woman may have encouraged the incipient feminism of H.G. Wells's mother and her schoolmates in the 1830s, but by the time of the queen's jubilees fifty and sixty years later, the gender of the monarch was of little real help to the aspirations of the developing women's movement. By this time the queen had come to stand for a domestic, familial and passive image of a woman, ruling, in her own expression, by example rather than by active participation in government. If the legal position of women in the country as a whole had in some ways improved during her reign, it seemed to have done so rather in spite of than because of the gender of the monarch.

Nevertheless, the presence of a female in the highest political position in the country had at times given strength, if only by implication, to the arguments of those of her female subjects who were seeking greater educational and political opportunities. Victoria was unique among married women in never having been subject to the law of coverture – that is, she was not obliged to take her husband's name or to hand over to him her property after their marriage. She was not prevented by marriage from entering into independent contracts or from disposing freely of her own property. From the 1870s onwards the laws governing married women's property began to be liberalized and by the end of the century women had seen their legal status improved in a number of ways. Divorce became available to the well-off through the law courts instead of only through private acts of Parliament, while legal separation offered some refuge for poor women from brutal and disastrous marriages. In general these concessions brought her female subjects some small part of the legal rights enjoyed by the sovereign and her presence and status must on occasion have helped the legal processes forward, whatever her own opinion on the questions.

In fact, of course, the projected image of placid and highly moral old age probably concealed the real extent of her daily concern with matters of state. 'The Queen *does* interfere,' Dilke complained in 1879, 'constantly.' During the Schleswig-Holstein dispute in the early sixties, when Prussia and Denmark were in fierce contention over the control of certain territories, it may well have been the queen's resolute determination to prevent conflict between Britain and Germany that prevented Britain from intervening in support of Denmark, and her continued affection for her first grandson, who became Emperor of Prussia in 1888, may have led him to underestimate the possibility of war with Britain and so have been a contributory cause of the First World War.

In domestic matters she increasingly distrusted radicals of all kinds, and her views certainly affected the composition of Gladstone's cabinets. Gladstone himself became in many ways more radical towards the end of his career, and in advocating a measure of home rule for Ireland and opposing the more militaristic and expansionist imperialist adventures, he earned a wide popularity among the urban working classes, but also the suspicion and even hostility of his sovereign. Whether he could have built on his popularity to bring about a moderate British liberal republic, as some people believe, must remain entirely hypothetical, since even when he was most exasperated by the monarch or her offspring, he remained an unshakeable royalist. When he died in 1898 Victoria recalled,

> He was very clever and full of ideas for bettering the advancement of the country, always most loyal to me personally, and ready to do anything for the Royal Family; but alas! I am sure involuntarily, he did at times a good deal of harm.

It is well known that the queen got on well with Disraeli and considerably less well with Gladstone. Her interest, however, was not confined to the purely subjective one of personal preferences among her statesmen. To the end of her life she took an active interest in all matters of state, demanded to be consulted and undoubtedly influenced many decisions. Her objection to Gladstone was the suspicion that his sympathy lay with high church, even Catholic groups within the church as well as his recklessness in matters of reform. She disliked his inclusion of radicals like Dilke, Bright and Chamberlain in his cabinet, but was also continually at odds with him over clerical appointments.

These latter meant very little to Disraeli, who allowed the queen her way on such questions, but with his gift for diplomacy and his genuine liking for women, managed to win the queen to his opinion on more important matters of state. Disraeli has gone down in history, probably rightly enough, as a great flatterer (for royalty, he is supposed to have said, it had to be laid on 'with a trowel'). Certainly the increasing identification of the throne with conservative politics which historians have noted during the last years of the nineteenth century owes a great deal to him. He never forgot that he was dealing with a woman as well as a monarch, and he helped to keep her gender as well as her status in the forefront of the royal public image. When he died in March 1881, the queen was devastated, and wrote to his secretary and friend Lord Rowton, 'Never had I so kind and devoted a minister and very few such devoted friends.' Disraeli himself, when asked as he lay dying whether he would like to be visited by the queen, replied, 'No, it is better not. She would only ask me to take a message to Albert.'

In her last years the queen did not become more cooperative or easier to work with than she had been in early life. She retained a violent temper and seems to have had the ability to reduce all around her, including her sons, to abject terror when she wished. Mary Ponsonby said that 'when she is disagreed with, even slightly, she thinks nothing too bad to say of the culprit'. Sir Henry Ponsonby, for more than thirty years her private secretary, was sometimes accused by other members of her household of failing to stand up to the queen. A gentle man with a quiet sense of humour, he recognized the problem. 'The fact is,' he wrote, 'that any advice I give to Her Majesty must be given in a most gingerly way.' He once described his method:

> When she insists that two and two make five I say that I cannot help thinking that they make four. She replies that there may be some truth

in what I say but she knows they make five. Thereupon I drop the
discussion. It is of no consequence and I leave it there, knowing the
fact. But X goes on with it, brings proofs, arguments and former
sayings of her own. No one likes this. No one can stand admitting they
are wrong, women especially; and the Queen can't abide it. Conse-
quently she won't give in, says X is unkind and there is trouble.

Ponsonby, like Disraeli, retained the queen's confidence and affection throughout his service. But he reminds us that the Victorian
legacy is not only that of the angel in the house, but also the moral
blackmailer and domestic tyrant of fact and fiction.

Before the publication of Lytton Strachey's study of the queen,
written in 1921, the general picture in the memory of the people of
Britain and the Empire was of Victoria in her last twenty years. On
the coins that they handled daily and in the public squares in their
towns and villages, a small, squat woman shaped rather like a
tea-cosy with an unsmiling face set in the grumpy lines of old age
represented the spirit of the nineteenth century. By the time she died
few of her subjects could remember any other figure on the throne;
few of the children who collected 'bun ha'pennies' for the Church
Missionary Society recalled that the queen who wore her hair in the
low Grecian knot which gave the coins their name was younger,
slimmer and more colourful than the old lady glowering at them in
bronze from the front of the town hall. Nor did the children who
repeated the song about the queen and the 'bonnie Scotsman' that
they heard the soldiers singing as they marched off to take part in the
world war take a lot of note of their parents' explanation of the story
behind it. In her later years Victoria was increasingly associated in
the public mind with unsmiling virtue and smug self-satisfaction.
The one phrase universally associated with her was 'We are not
amused'.

Whether because of this image of royalty, or in spite of it, by the
end of the nineteenth century the throne of Britain seemed as secure
as it has ever been throughout history. The queen's funeral in the
bitter winter weather of January 1901 was attended by loyal crowds
in London and Windsor, and her death was felt almost as a personal
tragedy by many of her subjects.

Victoria's final popularity and the stability she gave to the throne have been attributed by her biographers to her personal characteristics and qualities, but this is not really a convincing explanation. Few of her subjects had any way of judging the reality of her qualities. For example, the 'middle-class' image of the queen which was assiduously cultivated bears little relation to the actuality of her life. She travelled with an immense retinue of servants, ate off solid gold plates and had hands so weighted with jewels that on occasion she could barely handle her knife and fork. She was imperious in her choice of servants and attendants and caused a considerable amount of bad feeling among members of her household by importing several Indian servants, one of whom she promoted to the title of 'Munshi' (teacher) and accorded privileges above those of her regular household. The queen's relationship with the Munshi was that of a fond mistress and an over-indulged servant, harmless enough but demonstrating both her continued susceptibility to flattery and her occasional imperviousness to the advice and the feelings of her staff. It also illustrates the queen's apparent lack of racial prejudice. She incurred the anger or distrust of some of her advisers by the extent to which she took the Munshi into her confidence, and she strongly resented the prejudice shown to Indian and African visitors to her jubilee by some of her court. In 1874 she had written to the Earl of Carnarvon apropos of Bishop Colenso, who had translated the Bible into Zulu, expressing

> her very strong feeling (and she has few stronger) that the natives and coloured races should be treated with every kindness and affection, as brothers, not – as alas! Englishmen too often do! – as totally different beings to ourselves, fit only to be crushed and shot down!

Her lack of racial prejudice and her attitude to her servants distinguished her from the archetypal middle-class citizen of the period. There are many tales of her kindness to servants and to their children, towards whom, with the rest of her poorer subjects, she sometimes expressed a rather defensive attitude. She wondered 'why the clergy should go fussing about the poor or servants . . . The servants are very good people – why can't they be let alone?'

She was neither as philistine, religiose or snobbish as very many of her middle-class subjects, and indeed in some ways saw herself as being above class divisions. One observer, writing a few months after her death, considered that although she 'probably would not have signed a paper saying she believed in the divine rights of kings, in her heart she never questioned that she was the anointed of the Lord'.

Few of her subjects had any means of judging the reality of the queen's personality or the degree of her concern with matters of state. After her death even those near the centre of things continued to be surprised by the revelations brought by the passing years. The myth of the queen's political neutrality was destroyed as her letters began to appear in the years before the first war. The image of a mother-figure who stood in a kind of moral holy ground above the coarse realities of day-to-day politics was both an over- and an under-valuation of her character. But somehow, by the time of her death, the need of a figure on which to focus the idea of Britain had become so deeply part of the political scene that even republican political leaders feared to challenge it.

By 1931 Harold Laski, Labour's most important political theorist, was asserting that the Labour Party could not abolish the crown because it was far too popular. The best they could do was to demand the assurance that the throne be 'automatically neutral'. He looked back over the past century and recalling the dismissive, indeed abusive, tone in which *The Times* had announced the death of George IV, commented that

> any one who compares the comment of *The Times* upon the death of George IV with the national sympathy in the illness of George V can hardly regard the change in temper as other than a political miracle.

The miracle took place during Victoria's reign, above all in its last two and a half decades. It owes at least as much to those statesmen and others who worked at creating a royal image and a royal mother-figure in those years as it does to the personality of the queen herself. They succeeded in surrounding her with an aura of moral certainty and a strongly feminine quality of maternal devotion and disinterested family loyalty which impressed itself on subjects of many nations and many races. In doing this they diminished in some ways the actual woman, smoothing out her eccentricities and masking many of the contradictions of a complex individual, while in other ways raising her to almost superhuman status. Those who were

PRINCE OF WALES'
MARRIAGE.

Everybody stop and listen to my ditty,
And let the news spread from town to city,
The Prince of Wales has long enough tarried,
And now we know he has got married.

For he went to sleep all night
    And part of the next day,
The Prince of Wales must tell some tales,
    With his doo dah, doo dah, day.

His pastime for a week there's no disputing,
For the first three days he went out shooting,
He's like his father I don't deceive her,
And she like Vick is a good feeder.

The next two days, so it is said, sir,
He began to dig out the parsley bed, sir,
Like his dad he does understand,
And knows how to cultivate a bit.

The first day over he laid in clover,
And just alike he felt all over ;
At fox-hunting he's clever and all races,
Yet she might throw him out of the traces.

He must not go larking along with the gals,
Keep out of the Haymarket and Pall Mall ;
And to no married woman must he speak,
She'll stand no nonsense or half-crowns a-week.

In November next she must not fail
But have a little Prince of Wales,
Young Albert he must not be beat,
But contrive to make both ends meet.

When his wife is in a funny way,
Then he must not go astray ;
Of all those things he must take warning,
Nor go out with the girls and stop till morning.

The last Prince of Wales was a good'un to go,
He would ride with the girls in Rotten Row,
He use to flare-up, he was no joker,
He was as fat as a Yarmouth bloater.

He must look to his stock and cultivation,
He must be a father to the nation ;
He must begin to reap and sow,
Be a rum'un to look at, but a good'un to go.

He wants six maids as light as fairies,
To milk the cows and look to the dairy,
To his wife the household affairs confiding,
While the Prince of Wales goes out riding.

Long life to the Prince and his fair lady,
May she have health and bouncing babies,
May the Prince be King, we want no other,
And take the steps of his father and mother.

H. DISLEY, Printer, 57, High Street, St. Giles, London, W.C.

*Broadside commenting with some heavy irony on the marriage of
Bertie to Princess Alexandra of Denmark, 1863.*

consciously concerned with the projection of a popular royal image deliberately accentuated the non-political nature of the queen, making the distinction which Bagehot had pointed out in 1867, between the 'efficient' and the 'dignified' parts of the British constitution. The throne, Bagehot had insisted, was of the dignified part, whose function was, among others, to conceal the activities of the efficient. A monarch who was above politics served not only to unify differing interests, but to divert the public mind from the actual operation of the political and efficient parts of the constitution where real decisions were made.

If royal family expenditure continued to infuriate republicans and cynics, the saga of family occasions continued to fill the popular press and fascinate the general public. When the pathetic and degenerate elder son of the Prince and Princess of Wales died young in January 1892, heart-stopping accounts of his childhood saintliness were published, intended to 'go home to every parent's heart'. Letters of condolence to the queen came from women all over the country, including one from a group of miners' widows in Barnsley, recalling the queen's patronage of their relief fund after their husbands had been killed in a mining disaster some years earlier, and wishing 'it were in our power, dear lady, to dry up your tears and comfort you'.

In the later years of her reign, Mary Waddington noted,

> Queen Victoria had a great prestige in France. People admired in her not only the wise sovereign who had weathered successfully so many changes, but the beautiful woman's life as wife and mother. She was always spoken of with the greatest respect, even by people who were not sympathetic to England as a nation.

The power of an image that could win the French to an admiration for British royalty is self-evident. But another important element in the image-making of the last quarter of the nineteenth century was what Belfort Bax described as 'the rise and domination of Imperialism in politics . . . in the place of the old religious feeling'.

Modern generations living in a post-imperial world find it difficult to understand the imperialist ideology of the late nineteenth century. In an age in which all but an almost invisible handful of romantic reactionaries saw industrialization and urbanization as essential parts of the inevitable progress of humanity, politicians of all persuasions differed only as to the best way to bring the advantages of northern

European civilization to the backward parts of the world. Tories and
Conservatives favoured military conquest, Liberals relied on free
trade imperialism without formal conquest, while Fabians and many
other socialists favoured cooperative efforts to share enlightenment
and technological advance. That such advance was possible and
necessary was rarely questioned. Imperialism in one form or another
was part of the belief in progress and it had, as Bax said, taken the
place of older forms of religious belief. God was indeed called upon
to make Britain mightier than she already was, and to see that her
bounds were spread wider and wider, but the process was carried out
by a steady series of military actions each of which resulted in
another patch of red on the map and another outpost of British
authority.

A great deal of interesting historical work has been done in the
1980s about the process of royal and imperial consolidation in these
years. The image-builders who worked at popularizing the queen
were going with the grain of history, even if the extent to which the
process was consciously planned may be questioned. The increase of
empire and the increase of royal pomp and ritual went naturally
together, and the queen went along with both processes willingly.

Benjamin Disraeli was one of the great figures in the theatre of
nineteenth-century politics. He had an instinct for showmanship,
and he also had a strong appreciation of women as political actors.
He wrote to Lady Bradford in 1874, 'I must say I feel fortunate in
having a female sovereign. I owe everything to women.' In his novels
he often gave women characters not only the moral but the political
high ground, and characters like Sybil, the eponymous heroine of his
Chartist novel of 1844, and Theodora in *Lothair*, who a quarter of a
century later embodied the European revolutionary nationalist
underground, were presented as leaders and inspirers of political
movements. His conscious attempts to present Victoria to the world
after the ambivalent years of her early widowhood were carried out
with the intention of combining femininity with imperialism.

Disraeli has usually been credited with the creation of the title of
Empress of India, which marked a major point in the queen's return
to political visibility in 1876. It seems, however, that the idea was
one with which the queen was especially ready to fall in. She had a
very strong sense of precedence – indeed during the later jubilee

"NEW CROWNS FOR OLD ONES!"

(ALADDIN *adapted.*)

Punch *portrays Disraeli as a character from* Aladdin and His Wonderful
Lamp, *the wicked uncle who persuades Aladdin's mother to exchange the
magic lamp for a showy but worthless new one.*

celebrations her court officials had continually to consult her on such matters, since there seems to have been no one else in the world who actually understood all the intricacies of royal etiquette and precedence. However, in the early seventies she was annoyed to find that both the Emperor of Russia and the Emperor of Prussia claimed precedence (as emperors) over a mere queen, and thereby claimed precedence on royal occasions for their children over hers. The title of Empress, therefore, was something very much to be welcomed on that score alone. It was also the case that Victoria was always attracted by the exotic, and particularly by Indians and Africans. Mary Waddington complained of the profusion of maharajahs at the British court 'covered with gold and silver embroidery and diamonds and emeralds as big as eggs'. She objected that

> they always make a great fuss over the Indian Princes at Court – they treat them like Royalty and give them very good places. The Corps Diplomatique always protests.

To combine the title of Empress with a closer attachment to her Indian dominions, therefore, was very much to the queen's taste, and it was she who insisted on the title of 'Ind.Imp.' being added to the new coinage which was issued in 1886. Most of her ministers were dubious about the title, and originally insisted that it should be used only for correspondence with or involving India. But the queen rejoiced in the title and usually signed herself Victoria R & I (Regina et Imperatrix) after she had received it.

The queen's re-entry into public life was very much associated with the celebration of empire. In 1875 the Prince of Wales, at Disraeli's suggestion, had made a very successful tour of India, and the regular exhibitions held in London after the mid-century increasingly came to include artifacts and people from India, Africa and other parts of the colonial empire.

The images of empire were closely associated with the other image of motherhood and womanliness. Victoria came to be seen as not only ruler but mother of the nation. Her decision to continue to wear black after Albert's death probably helped to create a powerful image. Although she held resolutely to black as the colour of her dresses, she seems to have had no problem in loading herself with

jewels and diamonds, and she wore caps of white lace, sometimes
decorated with silver and diamonds, and white court feathers. The
resulting effect was dramatic and distinctive, especially in the usual
surroundings of public events in which most of the participants,
including the men, were wearing brilliant dresses and uniforms. At
the jubilee parade in 1887, the queen was dressed 'in black, with
silver embroidery, a white lace bonnet with feathers and lace caught
back by diamond pins', a considerably more graceful and striking

The Decorations · Every little helps · Hoisting the Standard

A TRUE LOYALIST.

"Little children grow to men :
Loyal *now* is loyal *then*."

REV. H. D. RAWNSLEY.

*Empire Day and jubilees were occasions for even the youngest to
demonstrate loyalty to the crown and the flag.*

form of dress than the garish colours and overblown flowers and jewellery which she had worn in Albert's time.

The queen's golden jubilee in 1887 and her diamond jubilee ten years later were celebrations of monarchy and empire. The processions blazed with exotic and colourful uniforms and costumes. The queen's picture decorated souvenir mugs for all schoolchildren as well as flags, bunting, plates, dishes, handkerchiefs and a huge range of commercially-produced merchandise, from chocolates and condensed milk to Colman's mustard. A recent writer has seen the jubilee years as ushering in the age of consumerism, with the royal image firmly planted on the mass-produced articles which celebrated its arrival.

The two jubilees certainly represented something quite new in the popular presentation of the monarchy. In 1887, to celebrate the golden jubilee, 30,000 children were entertained in Hyde Park with food, games, amusements and a decorated mug for each. The city was covered in greenery and bunting, there were 'flags, music and a general impression of movement and colour everywhere'. Mary Waddington took part, attending a reception at Buckingham Palace, and watching the colourful procession in which the queen and two of her daughters drove in an open landau, with the royal princes riding alongside on horseback. She thought 'the German Crown Prince superb, towering over every one else and his helmet shining in the bright sunlight'. This was Victoria's favourite son-in-law, husband of her eldest daughter, Vicky. Before the diamond jubilee was celebrated ten years later, he had inherited the title of German Emperor, but had died of throat cancer before he had ruled for a year, leaving his son Wilhelm II to reign in his place. Vicky herself was also to develop cancer, and to survive her mother by only a few months. If Vicky and her husband, Fritz, represented to some extent the practical and enlightened views of Victoria's uncle Leopold and of Albert, their son was more in tune with the end-of-century atmosphere of imperial expansion and competitive nationalism which was soon to lead to a major European war.

Victoria, by the time of her golden jubilee, was coming to be identified with the whole nation. Republicanism as a serious political issue had been shunted off into a siding, even by the supporters of the growing labour and socialist movements. It is true that there were those among the politicians and the royal family as well as among the reforming labour pioneers who still believed that there was not enough power or charisma in the end-of-century royal image to hold the public imagination. In 1891 for example, the queen's daughter Princess Louise thought it was time for her mother to abdicate:

> The people are learning to do without her and the government tell her very little, and she is reducing the future role of the Prince of Wales to a nonentity.

Keir Hardie thought the very exposure which the jubilees offered would demystify the throne:

> Royalty to be a success should keep off the streets. So long as the fraud can be kept a mystery, carefully shrouded from popular gaze it may go on . . . The light of day is too much for the mummeries on which the throne rests.

Both were wrong. The jubilees were welcomed by the people whom George Gissing satirized in his novel *In the Year of Jubilee* in the character of Mr Barmby:

> Now *I* look at it in this way. It's to celebrate the fiftieth year of the reign of Queen Victoria – yes; but at the same time, and far more, it's to celebrate the completion of fifty years of Progress. National Progress without precedent in the history of mankind! One may say, indeed, Progress of the Human Race. Only think what has been done in this half-century; only think of it! Compare England now, compare the world with what it was in 1837. It takes away one's breath!

But the celebrations were also welcomed by the huge crowds whose voice Gissing heard on the evening of Jubilee day:

> Along the main thoroughfares of mid-London, wheel traffic was now suspended; between the houses moved a double current of humanity, this way and that . . . But for an occasional bellow of hilarious blackguardism, or for a song uplifted by strident voices, or a cheer at some glaring symbol that pleased the passers, there was little noise; only a thud, thud, of footfalls numberless, and the low, unvarying sound that suggested some huge beast purring to itself in stupid contentment.

The jubilee celebrations were aimed at holding together the complex and often competing strands that made up the empire, the country and the metropolis. Nothing on this scale had ever been organized

HOME FROM THE PARK—THE JUBILEE MUG.

before. 'Biographies' of the queen stressed her goodness and the universality of her interests and concerns. An attempt was made to attach the sobriquet 'the good' to her title, but this did not take on. Parties were held, mugs were handed out to children and little but cheering was heard from the assembled multitudes. There were occasions, as when the queen drove to the East End of London to open the People's Palace as an educational and recreational centre, when some doubts crept in. The site was festooned with loyal messages such as 'Poor in District, your Presence makes us Rich in Affection' spelt out in flowers, but the queen reported, in a letter to Lord Salisbury, that she had heard 'a horrid noise *quite* new to the Queen's ears – booing she believes it is called' as she drove through the crowds. Archibishop Benson, who attended the occasion, recorded in his diary,

> The sight of those vibrating mighty ribbons of human faces and forms haunts the eye still, and I shall never forget it . . . it made one shudder at the thought of what would be, if ever those were against us.

But little hostility was manifest. Jubilee verses and hymns poured from the pens of male and female poets. Sir Arthur Sullivan composed a jubilee hymn to words by the Bishop of Wakefield:

> O Royal Heart, with wide embrace
>   For all her children yearning!
> O happy realm, such mother-grace
>   With loyal love returning!
> Where England's flag flies wide unfurled,
>   All tyrant wrongs repelling;
> God make the world a better place
>   For man's brief earthly dwelling.

A woman poet, Clara Thwaites, added her voice:

> O sons, brave sons, so stalwart, true and free,
> O daughters fair – a Woman's jubilee,
> A Sovereign's glad, imperial decree
> Calls with a clarion tongue, 'Rejoice with me!'

There were, of course, voices raised in protest at the jubilee revels. The small socialist journals and many liberal individuals who feared the raucous tones of imperialism and nationalism which the occasions brought forth, complained about the sycophancy and mindless junketing of much of the celebration. A writer in *Vanity Fair* saw Britain in decline as a world power and as a force for enlightenment in the world. Looking back over the fifty years' reign, the writer saw the record as a shameful one:

> Although in these fifty years we have waged only one European war (and that a war of collusion, when we were agreed with our enemy rather than our ally) we have waged a great number of wars in Africa

and Asia; wars for the most part unjust, waged without due cause, and
without Declaration of War.

On the morning of the diamond jubilee celebrations, Kipling
published his 'Recessional':

> The tumult and the shouting dies –
>   The captains and the kings depart –
> Still stands Thine ancient sacrifice,
>   An humble and a contrite heart.
> Lord God of Hosts, be with us yet,
> Lest we forget, lest we forget!

It ended with the couplet:

> For frantic boast and foolish word,
> Thy mercy on Thy People Lord!

When Victoria died early in 1901, she left the throne secure enough
to weather the accession of her son, whom Kipling described as 'a
corpulent voluptuary of no importance'. Her fears that his intellectual and moral limitations would discredit the crown proved un-
founded, and although he never reigned under the title she had asked
him to use, that of 'King Albert', he did nothing in his short reign to
diminish the solid edifice that her reign had established.

CONCLUSION

So all has been hushed up and Boehm lies sepulchred in the Abbey; and a memorial is being built for 'Victoria the Good' in front of Buckingham Palace, and the Queen's life is held up as a model for us all and for future generations.

Thus Wilfred Scawen Blunt wrote sarcastically in his diary, after recording the stories told him by Skittles about John Brown and other royal scandals. But by the time of her death the image projected by 'the old queen', as she seemed universally to be called in her last years and for several decades after her death, was more complex than this. Certainly the mourning at her death was widespread and almost universal. She had barely survived the century, and with her an era had passed away. But the values of her age, and to some extent her personality – at least its public image – already seemed to the young to be outdated, narrow, philistine, moralistic and prudish. For nearly half a century the word 'Victorian' was to be a term of dismissal, occasionally coloured only by a slight nostalgia for its implications of moral certainty. Most articulate people expected the new century to turn away from the old restraints and to bring liberation, expansion, toleration and a recognition of new possibilities of experience. Her successor was popular precisely with those in all classes of society who reacted against the moralism and domesticity of the Victorian image.

The passing years have shown the unfairness of the association of Victoria herself with the narrow and hypocritical attitudes to which her name came to be attached. She was a more complex personality, as modern scholarship has shown, and at times in her life stood against the weight of established power and authority. She gave her name to an era, but how far the age shaped the image which she left, or how far she impressed her personality on the age is impossible to gauge.

There is little doubt that the British monarchy was strengthened, stabilized and modernized during Victoria's reign. Many political and other aspects of British history helped to produce these effects. But in addition, three factors particularly relating to the queen's life made their contribution to the general direction of British politics during the era: her personality, her longevity and her gender. Twice during her sixty years' reign the crown appeared to be under threat, in each instance being threatened both from the 'right', by factions seeking to replace the queen with a more authoritarian, male figure, and from the 'left', by a perceived republican alternative. On both occasions – at the time of her accession and in the decade after her widowhood – republicanism was to some extent disarmed by the need to defend the queen against a less tolerable alternative, although this dilemma was clearly greater in the early period than in the 1860s.

Seen from a longer historical viewpoint, it could be argued that had the Hanoverian lobby succeeded in 1837 or the proponents of the queen's abdication in favour of her son in the 1860s, the short-term victory would have led to a rapid loss of support for the monarchy among liberal politicians and among the public at large, and therefore have made a British republic possible. This is pure speculation of course, but in both situations the fact that the monarch was a woman meant that she appeared less politically threatening to the opponents of monarchy itself and more amenable to constitutional control in the eyes of those who supported a limited monarchy. A female on the throne must always have appeared less 'political' in an age in which public political action was exclusively a male preserve.

In the same way, it is almost certainly the case that the non-English subjects were better able to accept a female head of state. The Scottish subjects had bitter memories of the Hanoverian kings and their military commanders, whilst the Irish had been forced into an unpopular union partly by the promise of Catholic emancipation which had then been refused by the Protestant bigotry of George III.

CONCLUSION   139

Neither country had any reason to feel loyalty to the Hanoverians,
but the young queen represented a break with the harshness of her
predecessors, and was able to regain the loyalty of the people of the
Celtic countries to a remarkable degree. In the later years a
matriarchal figure may also have been more acceptable to many of
the subject peoples within the empire, although the consideration of
this question goes beyond the scope of the present study. It remains
rather startling, certainly, to be told that to this day there are old
ladies in parts of India to whom the image of Queen Victoria remains
a cult figure.

If her gender made the monarch more acceptable as a figurehead
to the varied nations which made up her empire, it may also have
helped to popularize the throne in a way that was peculiar to the
nineteenth century. In earlier centuries the monarch was known by
name and perhaps by repute, but not until the nineteenth century
did the diffusion of cheap printed words and pictures bring the
image of the monarch and her family regularly into the consciousness
of her subjects. In the early years this was mainly a metropolitan
phenomenon, and for many subjects the picture on the coinage, the
postage stamps and perhaps an occasional piece of pottery would
present only a vaguely realized image. But as the reign progressed,
the royal family must have become familiar to a majority of their
subjects, in print and picture, and news of their activities spread
through the realm. By 1867 Bagehot considered that this trivial-
ization of the figure of the monarch was a source of strength. In a
famous passage he wrote,

> A *family* on the throne is an interesting idea. It brings down the pride
> of sovereignty to the level of petty life. No feeling could seem more
> childish than the enthusiasm of the English at the marriage of the
> Prince of Wales . . . But no feeling could be more like common
> human nature as it is, and as it is likely to be. The women – one half of
> the human race at least – care fifty times more for a marriage than a
> ministry.

Bagehot's picture is one that might well occur to a serious male
looking at the feminization of a once-powerful male symbol. It was
easier to place a female figure in a realm beyond politics, in an area
in which loyalty to the ruler became, even more than in earlier

centuries, synonymous with loyalty to country. By associating the throne with conservative politics, Disraeli and his successors completed a process which had been going on throughout the century towards attaching the concept of patriotism to the concept of conservatism.

In 1883, recalling Disraeli's career on the second anniversary of his death, *The Times* claimed that he had discerned 'in the inarticulate mass of the English population . . . the Conservative working man as the sculptor perceives the angel prisoned in a block of marble'. He had begun the liberation of this figure by the revival of a rhetoric of popular Toryism, but he had been assisted by a number of other developments.

The cheap press of the last two decades of the nineteenth century was quite different from the 'pauper press' of the earlier part of the century. It was centrally controlled, relied heavily on advertising and sought circulation by the presentation of sensational news items and the simplest of political appeals. At the same time as the mass commercial press was developing, commerce was taking over many forms of popular entertainment. The informal 'free and easys' of the beerhouses and pubs were being replaced by music halls run by national companies, offering large wages to performers who could entertain audiences in many different parts of the country. Nothing that might cause offence to established authority was permitted, and as safety regulations and other forms of licensing and controls made the small independent provincial hall more and more of an anachronism, the new commercial interests imposed new codes of conduct. Collins Music Hall, which flourished in Islington Green from the mid-sixties to the middle of the twentieth century, introduced for its *artistes* in 1892 regulations which stipulated that no offensive allusions were to be made to

> any member of the Royal Family; Members of Parliament, German Princes, police authorities or any member thereof, the London County Council or any member of that body; no allusion whatever was to be made to religion or any religious sect; and no allusion to the administration of the law of the country.

At the same time as the press and the sources of vulgar entertainment became more conservative, the state-regulated education system, which was consolidated after 1870, encouraged patriotic observances of all kinds, from daily prayers which included the queen and her family, to the regular annual observance of Empire Day, on which children brought their union jacks to school for a parade in the playground. When opposition liberal and later labour parties challenged the conservative hegemony of the last years of the nineteenth century, they found the people's royalism so deeply entrenched that they rarely tried to challenge it.

At the time of Victoria's accession she had asserted the right of a woman to succeed, and had shown herself well able to support the dignity of the role of monarch, more so indeed than her male predecessors. If she did not establish a clear female right to an active presence in conventional politics, she certainly reinforced those personal politics which had surfaced so strongly in the Queen Caroline agitation, the politics of the marriage contract and the authority of women's place in the family.

The nineteenth century, however, saw a move away from a view of the family as the centre of all life, including the life of work, towards an idealized family life of 'separate spheres', in which the lives of women and children were led in separate compartments and separate locations from the world of politics and the market place. For the poorer subjects, this was never more than a fiction, although it contributed to the loss of status of much work done by women. Among the middle and upper classes, however, by the mid-century there was some truth in Bagehot's picture of women whose whole concern was inward-turning. Those feminists who worked for the education of women and for their admission to the professions and other well-respected and well-rewarded work had to fight female as well as male prejudice to establish their case. For them, in the last decades of the century, there was little help in the image of the female monarch. After the death of her husband, Victoria refused ever again to wear the robes of state, appearing in versions – albeit on occasion jewelled and jetted versions – of widow's weeds. She opened Parliament on only six occasions after Albert's death, and appeared to the public increasingly as an elderly widow, concerned to protect the interests of her numerous family, rather than as a regal figure at the head of the nation. She made known her hostility to women's entry into the major professions, including medicine, and successfully concealed the extent of her own concern with the day-to-day politics of the country, allowing an image to be presented which was almost entirely domestic. As Bagehot had suggested, the idea of 'family' had become separated, perhaps almost opposed to, any idea of 'politics'. The family was women's sphere, and with it questions of affection and morality. In the rougher world of politics and trade, these sentimental areas could be disregarded or overridden and women's gentler and nobler natures were therefore unsuited to engage in such pursuits.

At the level of personal experience, a detailed study of Victoria's life and of her journals and letters could throw important light on the practical aspects of the doctrine of 'separate spheres' for men and women. As the one figure who escaped from the legal categories which governed male and female property-owners, and who in so many ways avoided the male/female gender roles, she was in her life torn between the public and private worlds. The successful figures in nineteenth-century public life at all levels gained their success on the basis of a strongly supportive system of private and family life. In this sector their children were born and brought up, their social relationships were maintained, their physical comfort was looked after, food was provided, prepared and set before them, clothes were made, laundered, repaired and cared for, but above all one figure, usually a wife but sometimes a parent or unmarried daughter, provided the total commitment and support which gave relief and sympathy to compensate for the harshness and competitiveness of the public world of work, politics or business.

For the wealthy, including the very wealthy monarch, some of this support could be provided by servants and staff. Nevertheless, there are some things which cannot be bought, and Victoria showed in her letters that she desperately needed the emotional support of a close and committed relationship. Her loss of her mother and her husband within months of each other left her bereft and unsupported, and she felt precisely the lack of anyone to whom she was supremely important in a personal sense. John Brown clearly supplied this need, which ordinary servants and young children could not fill, and after his death Princess Beatrice in many ways filled the classic role of the unmarried daughter whose life, in so many households, was sacrificed to a widowed parent's last years. It is true that the princess did marry, but her mother quite specifically insisted on a husband who was prepared to subordinate his own home life to hers, and who would allow the princess to be at her mother's constant command.

This function of the female – usually subordinate – part of the family was essential to the success of the Victorian male, and most of the success stories of men in public life were to a greater or lesser degree the story of supportive teamwork by wives and daughters as well as of the hero's success. Such a team was rarely dominated by a woman, especially as the century progressed and the professionalization of many occupations and the increasing legal complexity of business operations excluded those women who, in the late eighteenth and early nineteenth centuries, had sometimes been at the centre of successful professional and business enterprises – the founders of the Courtauld silk fortune in London, for example, or the Crossley carpet and textile fortune on the West Riding of Yorkshire. The century saw the pushing back of women into an exclusively domestic environment, both as an ideological trend and as a practical way of ensuring the maintenance of the male work force at all levels of urban and industrial society.

As a rare – in many ways unique – example of the female public figure at the highest level, Victoria illustrates the problems which such a role held for a woman. She had to produce her own children, supervise – however nominally – her own household, and maintain the moral command of the family. She clearly always wished to fulfil the female role. Her attachment to Albert made it possible for her to carry the two roles during his lifetime, although whether she would have deferred to him in political matters to the same extent when her children were older and her immediate family responsibilities less pressing cannot be known. After his death she made many compromises in the fulfilment of her public role, but never abandoned it. She remained superior to the men who governed the country and to her cousin George who for most of her life was commander-in-chief of the forces. Towards the end of her reign politicians and advisers tended to subsume the two roles into the one of 'mother' of the country and the empire, allowing the queen absolute control over matters of royal etiquette and such family questions as marriages and relations with the many royal houses which these involved.

Although the language of the private world was often used for the queen's duties and position, looked at objectively they were of the greatest public importance to the position of Britain in the world. The queen's life illustrated the possibility of role reversal, but also the very great difficulties which would confront a woman who wished to enter the world of work and politics while also bearing children and being responsible for a household. By the end of the nineteenth century women were beginning to enter some parts of the 'public' world, but for the most part only by assuming the social role of a man, that is by abandoning the maternal and familial roles, and by relying on servants or family members to provide domestic support. For all her own fulfilment of the two roles, the life and example of the queen, in the last years of her reign, gave much more support to the domestic view of women's role than to any suggestion that women should enter the world of active politics.

There are, of course, strict limits on the extent to which any individual can work effectively against the spirit of an age or the movement of opinion within it. Victoria was not a philosopher or a leader of thought and opinion. By holding the highest political office in one of the great powers of the world for sixty changing and eventful years, she inevitably presented her subjects with impressions, images and examples which must have had considerable effects. The images were contradictory, they changed over time and were open to more than one interpretation. In the early years of her reign, some radicals and reformers saw her as symbolizing a new, fresher and more liberal approach to government. By the end of her reign she represented ultra-conservatism in many ways, and although not allied to any political party, she left the monarchy closely associated with the most conservative elements in the politics of the time.

Victoria, nevertheless, was not associated with reaction in politics, and it should not be forgotten that within the royal household and in those of her children there were elements of serious concern which had more in common with aspects of the Fabian and liberal traditions than with the cruder politics of aggressive imperialism. The fact that she was a woman certainly helped to strengthen and stabilize the monarchy, and so to prevent the development in Britain of a more rational republican form of government. But she also kept a feminine presence in British public life in an age in which masculine dominion was in most areas strengthened. If she strengthened the moral authority of women in the family rather than making their presence in public life more immediately acceptable, there must have been many ways in which the presence of a woman at the head of the state worked at a deeper level to weaken prejudice and make change more possible in the century following her reign.

A NOTE ON SOURCES

SINCE this is a work of re-interpretation rather than new research I have relied in the main on the many published works about Queen Victoria for the narrative of events. Few of the incidents or events mentioned are contentious, so I have not footnoted every statement. Instead, a brief account of the main sources which have been used for each chapter appears in the notes that follow on pp. 155–63, where these have not already been explained in the text. I have added a list of the main non-royal diarists, writers and other informants whose work has been used by me and by other writers on pp. 152–4. Members of the royal family who appear in the book are listed on pp. xi–xii and the names of the prime ministers who served during the queen's reign with their political affiliations and the dates in which they held office are listed on p. xiii. Otherwise tables, genealogies and other lists have been avoided.

There is an enormous body of writing concerned with the queen. The writers have had access to a vast amount of manuscript material in the form of letters, memoranda and the queen's private journal. Victoria was a compulsive letter-writer, and her correspondence is a good illustration of the difference between the nineteenth century, when communications were rapid and efficient but the telephone was not available, and our own age. For example, in the years between the marriage of Princess Victoria in 1858 and the death of the queen in 1901 (which preceded that of her daughter by only a few months) 3,777 letters from the queen to her daughter survive and more than four thousand from daughter to mother. They contain the kind of exchange which today would take place on the telephone, and they provide both an enormous amount of detailed information about family and personal affairs and activities, and also an intimate and at times moving picture of a mother–daughter relationship. Such a record would be highly unlikely if not impossible today, when the mere act of committing things to paper rather than using a non-permanent form of communication would imply a self-consciousness and a deliberate awareness of posterity which are on the whole missing from this correspondence. There is evidence in the letters that both correspondents hoped that the letters would eventually be destroyed.

Victoria also kept a daily journal from her girlhood onwards. Extracts from this have been published, but unfortunately for historians the version which has been accessible is a 'weeded' one. The vast mass of personal correspondence and diaries which the queen and her family accumulated in the course of her sixty years on the throne was thinned out before biographers and other historians gained access to it. This illustrates, of course, the permanent tension which exists between the historian and the human being. The respect for the personal privacy even of the most highly paid and prominent of public figures must conflict with the historian's search for the truth of past events.

An account of the weeding that occurred of the papers of Queen Victoria and her family is given in Sir Philip Magnus's biography of Edward VII (London, John Murray, 1964, pp. 461 ff.) and reprinted in Cecil Woodham-Smith, *Queen Victoria* (pp. 436–7). In summary, it says that most of the personal correspondence of Edward VII, including all of that with his wife and with Queen Victoria, was burnt on the king's death in accordance with the instructions in his will. Before then Queen Victoria's manuscript journal had been taken over by her daughter Princess Beatrice, in accordance with her mother's instructions, and, selected passages having been transcribed, burnt. The journal which survives, and which has been so extensively used by writers, in fact consists of the selections which the queen had marked for her daughter to transcribe. There is also evidence that in the process of transcription after her mother's death, the princess made alterations of her own.

Among other papers which were destroyed were many other

batches of letters, including those of the queen to Disraeli (with the exception of some selected as being of 'political interest'), and those of Edward VII, when Prince of Wales, to Disraeli. All Queen Alexandra's papers were destroyed after her death by her lady-in-waiting and close friend, the Hon. Charlotte Knollys. Other manuscript material was consigned to the flames, including the diary of John Brown and the memoir of him which the queen wrote and intended to publish. These were burned by the queen's private secretary, Sir Henry Ponsonby.

Another manuscript source which seems largely to have disappeared is described by Queen Victoria's granddaughter, Princess Marie Louise, in her memoir *My Memories of Six Reigns*. She recalled that the queen, when she had anything unpleasant to say to any member of her family or household, whether or not they were in the same house at the time, would send a written note to the offender. The queen also seems to have been in the habit of writing instructions to family and servants which others might have delivered in person. These notes and instructions have mostly perished, although some avid collectors of memorabilia like Lord Edward Pelham-Clinton kept a few. Royal servants and others seem to have been more loyal and trustworthy than their modern counterparts, or perhaps were simply subject to fewer temptations. The Hon. Harriet Phipps, for instance, who was the queen's lady private secretary and Woman of the Bedchamber for many years, had all her papers and anything else connected with royalty, even signed photographs, destroyed on her death. A few items which had been in other than royal hands have surfaced from time to time, and where these have been quoted, specific reference is made in the text. Otherwise all quotations from and references to royal correspondence or journals refers to the published versions or to quotations cited in one of the major biographies.

I have consulted all the published extracts from the queen's journals and letters, the main ones being

The Girlhood of Queen Victoria, ed. Viscount Esher, 2 vols. (London, John Murray, 1912) which covers the years 1832–1840)

The Letters of Queen Victoria: A Selection of Her Majesty's

Correspondence Between the Years 1837–1861, ed. A. C. Benson
and Viscount Esher, 3 vols. (London, John Murray, 1907)

The Letters of Queen Victoria, second series 1862–1885, ed. George
Earle Buckle, 3 vols. (London, John Murray, 1926)

The Letters of Queen Victoria, third series 1886–1901, ed. George Earle
Buckle, 3 vols. (London, John Murray, 1932)

Queen Victoria in her Letters and Journals, ed. Christopher Hibbert
(London, Penguin, 1984). A biography constructed from extracts
from the queen's letters and journals; this contains the most
up-to-date account of the manuscript material

Barry St. John Neville, *Life at the Court of Queen Victoria, 1861–
1901*, (Exeter, Webb and Bower, 1984). Selections from the
queen's journals illustrated with pictures and ephemera from the
scrapbooks of Lord Edward Pelham-Clinton

I have also used the five volumes of the correspondence between Queen
Victoria and her eldest daughter, the Crown Princess of Prussia, edited
by Roger Fulford: *Dearest Child 1858–1861*; *Dearest Mama 1861–1864*;
Your Dear Letter 1865–1871; *Darling Child 1871–1878*; *Beloved Mama
1878–1885* (London, Evans Brothers, 1964–1981). A selection from
the correspondence between Queen Victoria and one of her Prime
Ministers is edited by Philip Guedalla in *The Queen and Mr Gladstone
1845–1898* (London, Hodder and Stoughton, 1933).

Queen Victoria herself published two volumes, *Leaves from the
Journal of Our Life in the Highlands* (1868) and *More Leaves from the
Journal of a Life in the Highlands* (1884). These are essentially edited
extracts from her journal, but edited in the years concerned by the
queen herself. They have been published in whole or in part in more
than one edition, including *Victoria in the Highlands*, ed. David Duff
(New York, Taplinger, 1969).

Autobiographies, diaries and volumes of correspondence have
been consulted, including the memoir by Princess Marie Louise
referred to (Harmondsworth, Penguin, 1959). Others are mentioned
in the source notes to the chapters in which they are used and in the
list of diarists and commentators on pp. 152–4.

There have been several exhibitions and published selections from the large and in many ways pioneering collection of royal photographs. Reproductions of many of these appear in the standard biographies. Unfortunately the queen herself appears to have considered it unsuitable for the monarch to be photographed smiling, so the image which the photographs represent of her are unfailingly serious.

An illustrated edition of Lytton Strachey's 1921 biography was produced to mark the 150th anniversary of Victoria's coronation. Published by Bloomsbury (London, 1987) it is edited and introduced by Michael Holroyd and contains many interesting contemporary prints, drawings and photographs. A selection of drawings and water-colour paintings is to be found in Marina Warner's *Queen Victoria's Sketch Book* (London, Macmillan, 1979) which presents impressive and rather endearing evidence of the queen's ability in these fields, although readers who remember *The Rose and the Ring* may suspect a contemporary reference in Thackeray's unkind picture of the princess's drawings. An illustrated volume *Queen Victoria's Dolls* published by permission during the queen's lifetime in 1894 has a series of charming coloured illustrations of her childhood toys, and is interesting both for the tone in which the queen herself is discussed, and perhaps even more for the assumptions about the lives, tastes and education of boys and girls which were accepted as commonplace in the last years of the century.

The exhibition of the work of Franz von Winterhalter which was put on at the National Portrait Gallery to celebrate the 150th anniversary of Victoria's accession gave the opportunity to experience the full impact of the skilful work of one of the ablest of nineteenth-century royal portraitists. Most of the items in the exhibition are excellently reproduced in the catalogue that was issued to accompany it.

A number of biographies and biographical studies of the queen, Prince Albert, Edward VII and other members of the royal family in the nineteenth century have been consulted. The most convincing and accessible biography of the queen herself remains Elizabeth Longford's *Victoria R.I.* (London, Weidenfeld and Nicolson, 1964). Cecil Woodham-Smith's uncompleted *Queen Victoria, Her Life and Times* (London, Hamish Hamilton, 1972) is a fuller account of the years up to 1861, while the most recent work, *Victoria, Biography of a Queen* by Stanley Weintraub (London, Unwin Hyman, 1987), adds some new information and corrects one or two errors in the light of more recently available material, but is neither as well nor as sympathetically written as the two earlier biographies.

Robert Rhodes James's *Albert, Prince Consort* (London, Hamish Hamilton, 1983) is essential reading as an accompaniment to a biography of the queen, and adds a great deal to an understanding of her life by giving a full and sympathetic picture of the husband whose influence was a crucial part of it. The 'official' five-volume biography by Sir Theodore Martin (London, Smith & Elder) published between 1875 and 1880 has more space for quotations from the prince's diaries and letters, but suffers from the inevitable limitations of the genre.

Most of the liveliest and most interesting work on those aspects of the queen and her reign which concern me has appeared in articles rather than in books. I am conscious of having gained a great deal from some of this work, and have tried to acknowledge this debt in the notes or in the text.

DIARISTS AND
COMMENTATORS

ONE of the chief sources for this sort of history is the published and unpublished letters and diaries of people connected with the court and the royal family. Since these are often referred to in the text simply by the name of the writer, the main ones are listed below with their dates and the chief published editions of their lives and works. I have consulted only the published versions.

1 Thomas Creevey MP
Politician and minor office-holder who kept a diary between about 1802 and 1838.

> *The Creevey Papers: A Selection from the Correspondence and Diaries of Thomas Creevey MP*, ed. H. Maxwell, 2 vols. (London, John Murray, 1903)

> *Creevey's Life and Times: A Further Selection from the Correspondence*, ed. John Gore (London, John Murray, 1934)

2 John Wilson Croker MP
Member of Parliament and government servant who also kept a diary.

> *The Croker Papers. The correspondence and diaries of John Wilson Croker*, ed. Louis J. Jennings, 3 vols. (London, John Murray, 1884)

> *The Croker Papers*, ed. Bernard Pool (London, Batsford, 1967)

3 Charles Greville
Another politician and minor office-holder who kept an extensive journal between 1814 and 1860. Just before his death in 1865 he

entrusted his friend Henry Reeve with the publication of his memoirs and diaries. These contained intimate details of the lives of politicians and of members of the royal family. The queen objected to material in them 'disparaging to her family' and Lord John Manners considered that it was as if 'Judas Iscariot wrote the private lives of the apostles'.

The Greville Memoirs 1814–1860, ed. Henry Reeve, 8 vols. (London, Longmans Green, 1874–1894)

The Greville Memoirs 1814–1860, ed. Lytton Strachey and Roger Fulford, 8 vols. (London, Macmillan 1938)

Leaves from the Greville Diary, ed. Philip Morrell (London, Eveleigh Nash and Grayson, 1929) contains a good one-volume selection

4 Baron Christian Frederick Stockmar

Prince Albert's personal physician and adviser, Baron Stockmar, was at court between 1837 and 1857. The memoir published by his son annoyed the queen in many ways.

Ernst Stockmar, Memoirs of Baron Stockmar (London, Longmans Green, 1879)

5 Sir Henry Ponsonby

The main such sources for the later part of Queen Victoria's reign are the journals of some of her ladies-in-waiting but above all the correspondence of the Ponsonby family. Sir Henry Ponsonby was her private secretary from the death of Prince Albert in 1861 until his last illness in 1895. For most of this time he kept up a regular correspondence with his wife Mary, and their letters and other family papers provide a day-to-day insight into aspects of the queen's life and her court in those years. Selections have been published, and the manuscript letters have been used by biographers. The Ponsonby papers consist of 117 boxes each containing 150 to 200 letters, 12 bound books of longer letters, memorandum books, diaries and packages of unsorted letters. Published material includes:

Arthur Ponsonby (Baron Ponsonby of Shulbrede), Baron Ponsonby, Queen Victoria's Private Secretary: His Life from His Letters (London, Macmillan, 1942)

Sir Frederick Ponsonby, *Recollections of Three Reigns* (London, Eyre & Spottiswoode, 1951)

F.E.G. Ponsonby (Baron Sysonby), *Sidelights on Queen Victoria* (London, Macmillan, 1930)

Magdalen Ponsonby, *Mary Ponsonby: A Memoir, Some Letters and a Journal* (London, John Murray, 1927)

6 Marie Mallet
Lady-in-waiting during the queen's last years.

Marie Mallet, *Life with Queen Victoria, Marie Mallet's Letters from Court 1887–1901*, ed. Victor Mallet (London, John Murray, 1968)

7 Edith, Countess of Lytton
Lady-in-waiting in the 1890s.

Lady Lytton's Court Diary, 1895–1899, ed. Mary Lutyens (London, Hart Davis, 1961)

NOTES

SOURCES FOR INTRODUCTION – ENGLAND IN 1837

I picked up the splendid list of Victoria's royal descendants from Caroline Chapman and Paul Raban, *Debrett's Queen Victoria's Jubilees* (London, Debrett's Peerage, 1977) which gives an excellent account in print and pictures of the jubilees.

For one example among many of a loyal woman subject's invocation of the queen in support of a feminist case, see Mrs J. Stewart, *The Missing Law, A Woman's Birthright* (1869). The first quotation from George Eliot is from *Felix Holt the Radical*, chapter 16. The opening chapters of this book give a wonderful recreation of the early 1830s in an English provincial centre, and reading the novel is a pleasurable way of gaining an insight into the nature of the politics of the time. It must always be remembered, however, that the account was actually written in the mid-sixties and bears many imprints of that period. The second quotation is from a letter to John Sibree, written in March 1848, in *Letters of George Eliot*, ed. Gordon S. Haight (London, Oxford University Press, 1954) vol. I.

The Disraeli extract comes from *Sybil; or, The Two Nations* (1845), book II, chapter 5. This is the most interesting of the contemporary novels dealing with Chartism, and the most perceptive treatment of the political questions. Like all Disraeli's political novels it is also well worth reading for its insights into the high politics of the period.

For a short account of Irish politics, including Catholic Emancipation and the Repeal Movement, see Robert Kee, *The Green Flag* (London, Quartet Books, 1976), vol. I, part III, or R.F. Foster,

Modern Ireland 1600–1972 (London, Allen Lane/The Penguin Press, 1988), part III.

For Chartism, see Dorothy Thompson, *The Chartists* (London, Temple Smith, 1984).

SOURCES FOR THREE PRINCESSES

For popular Jacobitism, see Nicholas Rogers, 'Popular Toryism and Jacobitism in Provincial Context: Eighteenth-Century Bristol and Norwich' in *The Jacobite Challenge*, ed. Eveline Cruikshanks (Edinburgh, John Donald, 1988) and *Ideology and Conspiracy, Aspects of Jacobitism 1689–1759*, ed. Eveline Cruikshanks (Edinburgh, John Donald, 1988).

The most recent account of the Queen Caroline agitation and of the propagandists and publishers involved is in Iain McCalman, *Radical Underworld: Prophets, Revolutionaries and Pornographers in London, 1795–1840* (Cambridge University Press, 1988). A good short account of the episode is Thomas Laqueur, 'The Queen Caroline Affair: Politics as Art in the Reign of George IV' in *Journal of Modern History*, 54 (1982). See also Craig Calhoun, *The Question of Class Struggle: Social Foundations of Popular Radicalism During the Industrial Revolution* (University of Chicago Press, 1982), and Iorwerth Prothero, *Artisans and Politics in Early Nineteenth-Century London* (Folkestone, Dawson & Sons, 1979).

The Byron lines are from *Childe Harold's Pilgrimage*, Canto 4, CCLXIC and CLXX. For Shelley, see Richard Holmes, *Shelley: The Pursuit* (London, Weidenfeld and Nicolson, 1974); for the Pentridge rising, see E.P. Thompson, *The Making of the English Working Class* (London, Gollancz, 1964). The Macaulay poem and letter are in *Life and Letters of Lord Macaulay*, ed. G.O. Trevelyan (first published 1876, Oxford University Press edition 1961), vol. 1. Miss Mitford's *Our Village* was published between 1812 and 1832.

SOURCES FOR THE THRONE OF ENGLAND

For a sympathetic and very readable account of the 'Wicked Uncles', see Roger Fulford, *Royal Dukes* (London, Duckworth, 1933), and of

George IV, J.H. Plumb, *The First Four Georges* (London, Batsford, 1956). There are many others, listed in the standard bibliographies. For the Duke of Kent, Mollie Gillen, *The Prince and His Lady* (Toronto, Griffin House, 1970) straightens out the details of his life before his marriage, including the story of the short life of his illegitimate baby daughter. Less respectable texts include Rt. Hon. Lady Anne Hamilton, *Secret History of the Court of England* (London, William Henry Stevenson, 1832) and John Banvard, *The Private Life of a King* (New York, Literary and Art Publishing Company, 1875). For a detailed examination of the Sellis case, see *The Trial of Josiah Phillips for a Libel on the Duke of Cumberland, and the proceedings previous thereto arising out of the suicide of Sellis in 1810. To which is added in an appendix, the republication of the pamphlet called 'A minute detail of the attempt to assassinate the Duke of Cumberland'* (London, Hatchard, 1833). In the latter pamphlet it is suggested that Sellis was a Jacobin and could have had a political motive for his crime.

The letter from Major Charles Jones is among the Jones papers in Manchester Central Reference Library.

The pamphlet *A Letter to the Queen on the State of the Monarchy* by 'A friend of the People' (1838) is attributed in the British Library catalogue as possibly by Lord Brougham. Napier's letter is from Sir William Napier, *The Life and Opinions of General Sir Charles James Napier* (London, John Murray, 1857), vol. 2.

Wells's account is from his *Experiment in Autobiography* (London, Gollancz, 1934), vol. 1.

SOURCES FOR VICTORIA AND ALBERT

There is a great deal about the royal relationship in all the biographies listed in the sources for the Introduction. The most recent biography of the prince, by Robert Rhodes James, contains a select bibliography of the main works. The official biography for which the queen made private papers available was the five-volume *Life* by Sir Theodore Martin (1875–80). There is a discussion of Prince Albert's finances in Winslow Ames, *Prince Albert and Victorian Taste* (London, Chapman and Hall, 1968). The anonymous *Private Life of the Queen, by a Member of the Royal Household* was published in 1898. A very interesting work which looks at the role her husband played as the queen's political adviser and describes the work of the private secretaries who held office after Albert's death is Paul H. Emden, *Behind the Throne* (London, Hodder and Stoughton, 1934); the letter from Albert to Stockmar and the description of the effect of Stockmar's training on the prince are taken from Emden.

Ethel M. Duff's *The Life Story of H.R.H. the Duke of Cambridge* (London, Stanley Paul & Co., 1938) is a life of 'George Cambridge', the queen's cousin and later her military chief of staff for most of his long life.

The story about 'no more fun in bed' may be apocryphal but it occurs in a number of places, usually without indication of its source. One place is the introduction by Barry St. John Neville to the account of *Life at the Court of Queen Victoria*, based on the papers of Lord Edward Pelham-Clinton, for some years Master of the Queen's Household.

Other family matters are discussed in Elizabeth Longford, 'Queen Victoria's Religious Life' in *Wiseman Review* 236 (Summer 1962) and the same writer's 'Queen Victoria's Doctors' in *A Century of Conflict*, ed. Martin Gilbert (London, Hamish Hamilton, 1966). There is more about the religious views of the royal couple in Walter L. Arnstein, 'Queen Victoria and Religion' in *Religion in the Lives of English Women 1760–1930*, ed. Gail Malmgreen (London, Croom Helm, 1986).

A marvellous essay in the invention of tradition which helps to explain the royal fascination with the Highlands is Hugh Trevor-Roper, 'The Invention of Tradition: The Highland Tradition of Scotland' in *The Invention of Tradition*, ed. Eric Hobsbawm and Terence Ranger (Cambridge, 1983); and see in the same volume, David Canadine, 'The Context, Performance and Meaning of Ritual: the British Monarchy and the "Invention of Tradition" *c*. 1820–1977'.

SOURCES FOR VICTORIA AND JOHN BROWN

The relationship between the queen and John Brown is discussed in all the biographies mentioned on pp. 153–155, and in other works

NOTES 159

about the queen and the court. Two books specifically on the subject are E.E.P. Tisdall, *Queen Victoria's John Brown* (London, Stanley Paul, 1938), from which I have quoted the mysterious letter, and Tom Cullen, *The Empress Brown: The Story of a Royal Friendship* (London, The Bodley Head, 1969), from which I have quoted the letter from the queen to the Brown family. Many of the stories which are in both books come from the Ponsonby material (p. 203), particularly *Recollections of Three Reigns*, and *Henry Ponsonby, Queen Victoria's Private Secretary*.

The Dean of Windsor's story is in G.K.A. Bell, *Randall Davidson, Archbishop of Canterbury* (London, Oxford University Press, 1952). The extracts from Scawen Blunt's diaries are from Angela Lambert, *Unquiet Souls* (London, Macmillan, 1984) and those from Sir James Reid's journal are from Michaela Reid, *Ask Sir James* (London, Hodder and Stoughton, 1987). This latter work contains a great deal of very interesting material about the queen and her family. The diaries and letters from earlier publications include those of Marie Mallet and Lady Lytton, and A.B. Cook and J. Vincent (eds.) *Lord Carlingford's Journal* (London, Oxford University Press, 1971).

Hector Bolitho, *Victoria the Widow and Her Son* (London, Cobden Sanderson, 1934) is also relevant for this chapter, and prints the interesting comment from Lord Clarendon. The question of the hereditary madness of the Hanoverians is discussed in I. Macalpine and R. Hunter, *George III and the Mad-Business* (London, Allen Lane/Penguin Press, 1969).

Contemporary journals cited are *Punch, The Times, Tinsley's Magazine*, and *Reynolds's Weekly Newspaper*. Modern news items include the *Observer* for 27 May 1979, for an account of a 'death-bed statement by a minister of the Church of Scotland', and *The Times* diary for 9 October 1985 for a reference to the diaries of the queen's physician, Sir James Reid, which were being edited after the death in 1972 of his son. Both news items hint at revelations yet to come.

The Victorian pamphlets cited are:

Brown on the Throne (London, Montague Smith, Chapman, Lee and Co., 1871) 23 pp.
John Brown, The Fortunes of a Gillie (London, Osborne and Roschone, 1867)

John Brown. A Correspondence with the Lord Chancellor; Regarding a Charge of Fraud and Embezzlement, Preferred Against His Grace the Duke of Athole, K.T. (London, printed and published by Alexander Robertson, 1873)

SOURCES FOR THE REPUBLICAN ALTERNATIVE 1 & 2

Republicanism in Britain has never had its own party, nor has it usually been a major item on the programme of any nineteenth-century party or movement. Perhaps for this reason, there is no single book on the subject, although Kingsley Martin, *The Crown and the Establishment* (1962) has a good and lively run-down of the recent history. There is also an account of the later part of the nineteenth century in E. Royle, *Radicals, Secularists and Republicans, 1866–1915* (Manchester University Press, 1980).

Most of the discussion is in articles, and I have used the following extensively for this chapter: John Cannon, 'The Survival of the British Monarchy', in *Transactions of the Royal Historical Society*, 5th series, no. 36 (1986); John Belchem, 'Republicanism, Popular Constitutionalism and the Radical Platform in Early Nineteenth-Century England', in *Social History* VI (1981); N. J. Gossman, 'Republicanism in Nineteenth-Century England', in *International Review of Social History* VII (1962); Royden Harrison, 'The Republicans: A Study of the Proletarian Left 1869–73', in his *Before the Socialists* (London, Routledge & Kegan Paul, 1965); F. D'Arcy, 'Charles Bradlaugh and the English Republican Movement 1868–78', in *Historical Journal* XXV (1982).

Most of the politicians mentioned have been the subject of a number of political and biographical studies. Those I have quoted from here include S. Gwynn and G.M. Tuckwell, *The Life of the Rt. Hon. Sir Charles W. Dilke* (London, John Murray, 1917); J.L. Garvin, *The Life of Joseph Chamberlain* (London, Macmillan, 1932); William Stewart, *A Biography of J. Keir Hardie* (London, Waverley Book Co., 1921) and Fred Reid, *Keir Hardie, The Making of a Socialist* (London, Croom Helm, 1978); F.B. Smith (for W.B. Linton) *Radical Artisan* (Manchester University Press, 1973), and E.P. Thompson, *William Morris, Romantic to Revolutionary* (London, Lawrence and Wishart,

1955). John Bright made a number of statements against republicanism; the one cited comes from *The Public Letters of the Rt. Hon. John Bright MP*, collected and edited by H.J. Leech (London, Sampson Low, 1885). There is also material in Edward Royle, *Victorian Infidels* (Manchester University Press, 1974). The incident of the unemployed church occupation is from Hugh McLeod, *Class and Religion in the Late Victorian City* (London, Croom Helm, 1974). The incident of Edward Carpenter's interview for the post of royal tutor is in Ben Pimlott's *Hugh Dalton: A Biography* (London, Cape, 1985), which also gives an account of the career of Canon Dalton who in fact occupied the post.

Contemporary sources quoted are Thomas Paine, *The Rights of Man* (1792); Peter Murray McDouall, *McDouall's Chartist and Republican Journal* (1841), and *Dr P.M. McDouall's Poetical Petition to Queen Victoria on Behalf of the Oppressed Working Classes of Great Britain and Ireland, and in Demand of Their Political Rights and Liberty* (Liverpool, 1849); *The National Petition of the Industrious Classes* (Leeds, Hobson, 1842); Ernest Jones, 'The New World; or, The Revolt of Hindostan', in *Poems and Notes to the People*, no. 1, (1851) and *Democracy Vindicated* (1867); ed. W.J. Linton, *The English Republic*; [pseud.] Solomon Temple, Builder [possibly George Otto Trevelyan], *What does she do with it?* (1871); Charles Bradlaugh, *The Impeachment of the House of Brunswick* (first edn. 1871, reissued London, Freethought Publishing Co., 1883, reprinted in *A Selection of Political Pamphlets of Charles Bradlaugh* with preface and bibliographical notes by John Saville, New York, Augustus M. Kelley, 1970); William Morris, *Commonweal* (1887). For a selection from British writing in support of the Paris Commune, see *The English Defence of the Commune*, ed. Royden Harrison (London, Merlin Press, 1971). W.E. Adams's autobiography is *Memoirs of a Social Atom* (London, Hutchinson, 1903). Walter Bagehot *The English Constitution* (1867, reprinted with introduction by R.H.S. Crossman, London, Watts, 1964) gives the 'classical' account of the Victorian monarchy, from which I have quoted here and later. For a critique of Bagehot and a contemporary bash at monarchism, see Tom Nairn, *The Enchanted Glass* (London, Verso, 1988).

SOURCES FOR JUBILEE YEARS

The best account of the queen in these years is in Elizabeth Longford *Victoria R.I.* (London, Weidenfeld and Nicolson, 1964). There is a very lively account of the 1887 golden jubilee in the opening chapter of Stanley Weintraub's *Victoria, Biography of a Queen* (London, Unwin Hyman, 1987). Probably the best descriptive account, put together from contemporary material of many kinds, is Caroline Chapman and Paul Raban, *Debrett's Queen Victoria's Jubilees* (London, Debrett's Peerage, 1977). A very detailed account of the arrangements can be found in Jeffrey I. Lant, *Insubstantial Pageant: Ceremony and Confusion at Queen Victoria's Court* (New York, Taplinger, 1980). This is only a small selection from the enormous literature on these years.

There are very many accounts of the queen and of the jubilees in published reminiscences and memoirs. I have used those of Mary Waddington, American wife of the French ambassador at the Court of St James, published in two volumes: *My Years as a Frenchwoman* (London, Smith Elder, 1914) and *Letters of a Diplomat's Wife* (London, Smith Elder, 1905), which give something of an insider's view of the events.

For political questions, Frank Hardie, *The Political Influence of Queen Victoria* (London, Oxford University Press, 1935) opened up a serious examination of the question. There is more in the Guedalla Gladstone volumes, and in R. Shannon's biography *Gladstone* (London, Hamish Hamilton, 1982), although this has so far only taken the story as far as 1865. It does, however, make the interesting suggestion that Gladstone had begun to get on well with Albert, which adds the possibility that another door was closed by the prince's early death.

Disraeli is very well documented. The very full modern biography by Robert Blake, *Disraeli* (London, Eyre and Spottiswoode, 1966), is the most accessible, but Theo Aranson's *Victoria and Disraeli* (London, Cassell, 1977) has some material in addition about the queen, and the six-volume biography by Moneypenny and Buckle, *Life of Disraeli* (London, John Murray, 1929) has more space for letters and other comments.

The assessment of imperialism is from E. Belfort Bax, *Reminiscences and Reflexions of a Mid and Late Victorian* (London, Allen and Unwin, 1918), and the discussion of the monarchy by Laski may be found in his *Democracy in Crisis* (London, George Allen & Unwin, 1933) and *The Labour Party and the Constitution* (London, The Fabian Society, 1931).

George Gissing's *In the Year of Jubilee*, first published in 1894, was reissued in an Everyman edition in 1947. Contemporary non-literary celebrations are described and illustrated in Robert Opie, *Rule Britannia: Trading on the British Image* (Harmondsworth, Penguin, 1985) and John May, *Victoria Remembered* (London, Heinemann, 1983). This latter shows the images and mementoes from her reign up until the death of Albert.

There is a huge literature on imperialism, but see in this connection *Imperialism and Popular Culture*, ed. J.M. Mackenzie (Manchester University Press, 1984), especially the chapter by Penny Summerfield, 'Patriotism and Empire: Music Hall Entertainment 1870–1914)', from which the Collins' prohibitions are taken, and the early chapters of John M. Mackenzie, *Propaganda and Empire: The Manipulation of British Public Opinion, 1880–1961* (Manchester University Press, 1984).

Two articles to which I have referred, among the very many consulted, are John Davies, 'Victoria and Victorian Wales', in *Politics and Society in Wales 1840–1922*, ed. Geraint H. Jenkins and J. Beverly Smith (Cardiff, University of Wales Press, 1988), and Thomas Richards, 'The Image of Victoria in the Year of Jubilee', in *Victorian Studies*, vol. 31, no. 1 (Autumn 1987). Most of the contemporary material quoted comes from these sources, or from *Commonweal*, *The Times* and *The Labour Leader*.

A fair example of contemporary hagiography from which a number of illustrations are taken is Charles Bullock, B.D., *The Queen's Resolve* (London, 'Home Words' publishing office, 1897).

INDEX

WILLA CATHER

A Life Saved Up

Hermione Lee

Willa Cather is one of the great American writers of this century. Her fiction charts new, female versions of epic pioneering heroism and the extraordinary cultural encounters of 'New World' history. Cather is usually read as a nostalgic celebrator of American pastoral. Hermione Lee's major reinterpretation of her work explores that American context and those traditions, but finds a stranger and more disconcerting Cather: a writer of split identities, sexual conflict, dramatic energies and stoic fatalism.

Born in Virginia in 1873, Willa Cather was uprooted in childhood to the newly settled prairies of Nebraska. This startling transition profoundly coloured her life and work. Her strongest feelings were directed towards women, and her friendships – from Sarah Orne Jewett and Dorothy Canfield to Stephen Tennant and Yehudi Menuhin – were of deep importance to her. Yet as she became more famous, she withdrew increasingly from a modern world she disliked.

Travelling beneath the apparently simple surface of Cather's work, Hermione Lee presents an illuminating and exciting new reading of this marvellous writer.

EMILY DICKINSON

Helen McNeil

Today Emily Dickinson (1830 – 86) is gaining her deserved place alongside Walt Whitman as one of the two great American poets of the nineteenth century. From 1854 until her death, she lived almost exclusively in the small New England town of Amherst, a recluse who saw only ten of her 1,700 or so poems published in her lifetime. She remained largely unacknowledged until the publication of her *Complete Poems* in 1955. Now Helen McNeil brilliantly assesses the grounds for and the meaning of her belated recognition, She argues that not only was Dickinson's reclusiveness a strategy for asking forbidden questions, but that the absence of a readership during her lifetime gave her poetry its unique freedom and stature. In an era when women were encouraged to write only so long as they wrote badly or sentimentally, Dickinson's isolation permitted her to decide for herself what poetry could be about and what kind of language it could use. In this impressive study of her life and work, Helen McNeil both celebrates her individuality and shows how the English poetic tradition is altered by an understanding of Dickinson's accomplishment.

GEORGE ELIOT

Jennifer Uglow

One of the most brilliant writers of her day, George Eliot (1819 – 1880) was also one of the most talked about. Born Mary Ann Evans in the Midlands, she lost her faith and her family in a lonely struggle for learning. She lived – unmarried – with George Lewes from 1854 until his death in 1878: intellectual and independent, she had the strength of spirit to defy polite society with her highly unorthodox private life. So why did she apparently deny her fictional heroines the same opportunities? In this detailed and thought-provoking appraisal of her life and work, Jennifer Uglow explores George Eliot's ambivalent attitude to choice and change, especially for women, and illustrates how Eliot confronts the inner tensions of central images of Victorian life, such as class allegiance and the woman's role, to create a vision of a more generous way of life inspired by the imagination and the power of feeling.

THE DARKENED ROOM

Women, Power and Spiritualism in Late Victorian England

Alex Owen

This brilliant and highly original study looks at the central role played by women as mediums, healers and believers during the 'golden age' of British spiritualism in the late Victorian era. The movement, which maintained that women were uniquely qualified to commune with spirits of the dead, offered mediums a new independence and authority which, while privileging so-called feminine virtues, was capable of undermining conventional class and gender relations and redefining the nature of women's power in both the home and society.

The seance, whether treated seriously as a science or regarded as an amusing parlour game, enthralled large sections of society, invoking a startling world of darkened rooms, locked cabinets, mischievous and theatrical apparitions and moving episodes of happiness lost and regained, and gave to public and private practitioners an influence remarkable for their time. But the personal costs were sometimes high, and many spiritualists suffered badly at the hands of the medical and legal establishment.

Using hitherto unexamined sources, and incorporating analysis, theory and the telling of wonderful tales – what the author calls 'black and white with technicolour' – Alex Owen traces the movement's links with evangelical Christianity, with power structures based on class and gender, women's emancipation, faith healing and emergent psychiatry. At once scholarly and hugely entertaining, it provides fascinating new insight into women's place in Victorian, and spiritualist, society.

EVER YOURS, FLORENCE NIGHTINGALE

Selected Letters

Edited by Martha Vicinus and Bea Nergaard

For many, Florence Nightingale is the most famous woman of her day after Queen Victoria. Adulated by the public and her friends, considered an irritant by most politicians and bureaucrats, she remains a figure of considerable controversy. Unlike other historical accounts of her life and work, *Ever Yours, Florence Nightingale* presents this great pioneer in her own words: from the welter of surviving letters – of which there are over ten thousand – the editors have selected a fascinating range which captures in one volume Florence Nightingale's public and personal self. We see the child at eight, primly measuring her acts of naughtiness and kindness in letters to her mother, the young woman who discussed religion and philosophy with her father, and the zealous, indefatigable reformer who, despite taking to her bed after her return from the Crimea, wrote endlessly, advising, abjuring, hectoring, consoling both those in the public world and the private. What her letters show her to be is a woman of great brilliance and contradiction – stubborn and inspiring, witty and impatient, dedicated and meddling – who influenced not only her own age, but also subsequent generations.